WALKS IN
PROVENCE

Titles in the Footpaths of Europe Series

Normandy and the Seine
Walking through Brittany
Walks in Provence
Coastal Walks: Normandy and Brittany
Walking the Pyrenees
Walks in the Auvergne

WALKS IN
PROVENCE

Translated by Robyn Marsack
Translation co-ordinator Ros Schwartz

Robertson McCarta

The publishers thank the following people for their help with this book: Isabelle Daguin, Philippe Lambert, Vicky Hayward, Gianna Rossi, Eileen Cadman

First published in 1989 by

Robertson McCarta Limited
122 King's Cross Road,
London WC1X 9DS

in association with

Fédération Française de Randonnée Pédestre
8 Avenue Marceau
75008 Paris

© Robertson McCarta Limited
© Fédération Française de Randonnée Pédestre
© Maps, Institut Geographique National (French Official Survey)
  and Robertson McCarta Limited.

Managing Editor Jackie Jones
Designed by Prue Bucknall
Production by Grahame Griffiths
Typeset by Columns of Reading
Planning Map by Robertson Merlin

Printed and bound in Hong Kong

British Library Cataloguing in Publication Data

Walks in Provence — (Footpaths of Europe)
  1. France. Côte d'Azur & Provence, Visitor's guide
  914–4'904838
  ISBN—85365—150—8

CONTENTS

A note from the publisher

The books in this French Walking Guide series are published in association and with the help of the Fédération Française de la Randonnée Pédestre (French ramblers' association) — generally known as the FFRP.

The FFRP is a federal organisation and is made up of regional, local and many other associations and bodies that form its constituent parts. Individual membership is through these various local organisations. The FFRP therefore acts as an umbrella organisation overseeing the waymarking of footpaths, training and the publishing of the *Topo-guides*, detailed guides to the Grande Randonnée footpaths.

There are at present about 170 Topoguides in print, compiled and written by local members of the FFRP, who are responsible for waymarking the walks — so they are well researched and accurate.

We have translated the main itinerary descriptions, amalgamating and adapting several *Topo-guides* to create new regional guides. We have retained the basic *Topo-guide* structure, indicating length and times of walks, and the Institut Géographique National (official French survey) maps overlaid with the routes.

The information contained in this guide is the latest available at the time of going to print. However, as publishers we are aware that this kind of information is continually changing and we are anxious to enhance and improve the guides as much as possible. We encourage you to send us suggestions, criticisms and those little bits of information you may wish to share with your fellow walkers. Our address is: Robertson-McCarta, 122 King's Cross Road, London WC1X 9DS.

We shall be happy to offer a free copy of any one of these books to any reader whose suggestions are subsequently incorporated into a new edition.

It is possible to create a variety of routes by referring to the walks above and to the planning map (inside the front cover). Transport and accommodation are listed in the alphabetical index at the back of the book.

KEY

Gournay

This example shows that it is 7km from Gournay to Arbois, and that you can expect it to take 2 hours, 10 minutes.

7Km
2:10

ARBOIS
⌂ ▲ ✕ ⚏ ▭
14th century church

Arbois has a variety of facilities, including hotels and buses. Hotel addresses and bus/train connections may be listed in the index at the back of the book.

a grey arrow indicates an alternative route that leaves and returns to the main route.

Detour

indicates a short detour off the route to a town with facilities or to an interesting sight.

Symbols:

⌂ hotel;
⌂ youth hostel, hut or refuge;
▲ camping;
✕ restaurant;
♀ cafe;

⚏ shops;
▄ railway station;
▭ buses;
⚓ ferry;
ⓑ tourist information.

THE FOOTPATHS OF FRANCE

by Robin Neillands

Why should you go walking in France? Well, walking is fun and as for France, Danton summed up the attractions of that country with one telling phrase: 'Every man has two countries,' he said, 'his own . . . and France.' That is certainly true in my case and I therefore consider it both a pleasure and an honour to write this general introduction to these footpath guides to France. A pleasure because walking in or through France is my favourite pastime, an honour because these excellent English language guides follow in the course set by those Topo-guides published in French by the Fédération Française pour la Randonnée Pédestre, which set a benchmark for quality that all footpath guides might follow. Besides, I believe that good things should be shared and walking in France is one of the most pleasant activities I know.

I have been walking in France for over thirty years. I began by rambling — or rather ambling — through the foothills of the Pyrenees, crossing over into Spain past the old Hospice de France, coming back over the Somport Pass in a howling blizzard, which may account for the fact that I totally missed two sets of frontier guards on both occasions. Since then I have walked in many parts of France and even from one end of it to the other, from the Channel to the Camargue, and I hope to go on walking there for many years to come.

The attractions of France are legion, but there is no finer way to see and enjoy them than on foot. France has two coasts, at least three mountain ranges — the Alps, Pyrenees and the Massif Central — an agreeable climate, a great sense of space, good food, fine wines and, believe it or not, a friendly and hospitable people. If you don't believe me, go there on foot and see for yourself. Walking in France will appeal to every kind of walker, from the day rambler to the backpacker, because above all, and in the nicest possible way, the walking in France is well organized, but those Francophiles who already know France well, will find it even more pleasureable if they explore their favourite country on foot.

The GR system

The Grande Randonnée (GR) footpath network now consists of more than 40,000 kilometres (25,000 miles) of long-distance footpath, stretching into every part of France, forming a great sweep around Paris, probing deeply into the Alps, the Pyrenees, and the volcanic cones of the Massif Central. This network, the finest system of footpaths in Europe, is the creation of that marvellously named organization, la Fédération Française de Randonnée Pédestre, Comité National des Sentiers de Grande Randonnée, which I shall abbreviate to FFRP-CNSGR. Founded in 1948, and declaring that, 'un jour de marche, huit jours de santé,' the FFRP-CNSGR has flourished for four decades and put up the now familiar red-and-white waymarks in every corner of the country. Some of these footpaths are classic walks, like the famous GR65, Le Chemin de St Jacques, the ancient Pilgrim Road to Compostela, the TMB, the Tour du Mont Blanc, which circles the mountain through France, Switzerland and Italy, or the 600-mile long GR3, the Sentier de la Loire, which runs from the Ardèche to the Atlantic, to give three examples from the hundred or so GR trails available. In addition there is an abundance of GR du Pays or regional footpaths, like the Sentier de la Haute Auvergne, and the *Sentier Tour des Monts d'Aubrac*. A 'Tour', incidentally, is usually a circular walk. Many of these regional or provincial GR trails are charted and waymarked in red-and-yellow by local outdoor organisations such as ABRI (Association Bretonne des Relais et Itineraires) for Brittany, or CHAMINA for the Massif Central. The walker in France will soon become familiar with all these footpath networks, national, regional or local, and find them the perfect way into the heart and heartland of France. As a little bonus, the GR networks are expanding all the time, with the detours — or *varientes* — off the main route eventually linking with other GR paths or *varientes* and becoming GR trails in their own right.

Walkers will find the GR trails generally well marked and easy to follow, and they have two advantages over the footpaths commonly encountered in the UK. First, since they are laid out by local people, they are based on intricate local knowledge of the local sights. If there is a fine view, a mighty castle or a pretty village on your footpath route, your footpath through France will surely lead you to it. Secondly, all French footpaths are usually well provided with a wide range of comfortable country accommodation, and you will discover that the local people, even the farmers, are well used to walkers and greet them with a smile, a '*Bonjour*' and a '*bon route*'.

Terrain and Climate

As a glance at these guides or any Topo-guide will indicate, France has a great variety of terrain. France is twice the size of the UK and many natural features are also on a larger scale. There are three main ranges of mountains: the Alps contain the highest mountain in Europe, the Pyrenees go up to 10,000 ft, the Massif Central peaks to over 6000 ft, and there are many similar ranges with hills which overtop our highest British peak, Ben Nevis. On the other hand, the Auvergne and the Jura have marvellous open ridge walking, the Cévennes are steep and rugged, the Ardèche and parts of Provence are hot and wild, the Ile de France, Normandy, Brittany and much of Western France is green and pleasant, not given to extremes. There is walking in France for every kind of walker, but given such a choice the wise walker will consider the complications of terrain and weather before setting out, and go suitably equipped.

France enjoys three types of climate: continental, oceanic and mediterranean. South of the Loire it will certainly be hot to very hot from mid-April to late September. Snow can fall on the mountains above 4,000 ft from mid-October and last until May, or even lie year-round on the tops and in couloirs; in the high hills an ice-axe is never a frill. I have used one by the Brêche de Roland in the Pyrenees in mid-June.

Wise walkers should study weather maps and forecasts carefully in the week before they leave for France, but can generally expect good weather from May to October, and a wide variety of weather — the severity depending on the terrain — from mid-October to the late Spring.

Accommodation

The walker in France can choose from a wide variety of accommodation with the assurance that the walker will always be welcome. This can range from country hotels to wild mountain pitches, but to stay in comfort, many walkers will travel light and overnight in the comfortable hotels of the *Logis de France* network.

Logis de France The *Logis de France* is a nationwide network of small, family-run country hotels, offering comfortable accommodation and excellent food. *Logis* hotels are graded and can vary from a simple, one-star establishment, with showers and linoleum, to a four- or five-star *logis* with gastronomic menus and deep-pile carpets. All offer excellent value for money, and since there are over 5,000 scattered across the French countryside, they provide a good focus for a walking day. An annual guide to the *Logis* is available from the French Government Tourist Office, 178 Piccadilly, London W1V 0AL, Tel. (01) 491 7622.

Gites d'Etape: A *gîte d'étape* is best imagined as an unmanned youth hostel for outdoor folk of all ages. They lie all along the footpath networks and are usually signposted or listed in the guides. They can be very comfortable, with bunk beds, showers, a well equipped kitchen, and in some cases they have a warden, a *guardien*, who may offer meals. *Gîtes d'étape* are designed exclusively for walkers, climbers, cyclists, cross country skiers or horse-riders. A typical price (1989) would be Fr.25 for one night. *Gîtes d'étape* should not be confused with a *Gîte de France*. A *gîte* — usually signposted as '*Gîte de France*' — is a country cottage available for a holiday let, though here too, the owner may be more than willing to rent it out as overnight accommodation.

Youth hostels: Curiously enough, there are very few Youth Hostels in France outside the main towns. A full list of the 200 or so available can be obtained from the Youth Hostel Association (YHA), Trevelyan House, St Albans, Herts AL1 2DY.

Pensions or cafes: In the absence of an hotel, a *gîte d'étape* or a youth hostel, all is not lost. France has plenty of accommodation and an enquiry at the village cafe or bar will usually produce a room. The cafe/hotel may have rooms or suggest a nearby pension or a *chambre d'hôte*. Prices start at around Fr.50 for a room, rising to, say, Fr.120. (1989 estimate).

Chambres d'hôte: A *chambre d'hôte* is a guest room or, in English terms, a bed-and-breakfast, usually in a private house. Prices range up from about Fr.60 a night. *Chambres d'hôte* signs are now proliferating in the small villages of France and especially if you can speak a little French are an excellent way to meet the local people. Prices (1989) are from, say, Fr.70 a night for a room, not per person.

Abris: *Abris*, shelters or mountain huts can be found in the mountain regions, where they are often run by the *Club Alpin Français*, an association for climbers. They range from the comfortable to the primitive, are often crowded and are sometimes reserved for members. Details from the Club Alpin Français, 7 Rue la Boétie, Paris 75008, France.

Camping: French camp sites are graded from one to five star, but are generally very good at every level, although the facilities naturally vary from one cold tap to shops, bars and heated pools. Walkers should not be deterred by a '*Complet*' (Full) sign on the gate or office window: a walker's small tent will usually fit in somewhere. *Camping à la ferme*, or farm camping, is increasingly popular, more primitive — or less regimented — than the official sites, but widely available and perfectly adequate. Wild camping is officially not permitted in National Parks, but unofficially if you are over 1,500m away from a road, one hour's walk from a *gîte* or campsite, and where possible ask permission, you should have no trouble. French country people will always assist the walker to find a pitch.

The law for walkers

The country people of France seem a good deal less concerned about their 'rights' than the average English farmer or landowner. I have never been ordered off land in France or greeted with anything other than friendliness . . . maybe I've been lucky. As a rule, walkers in France are free to roam over all open paths and tracks. No decent walker will leave gates open, trample crops or break down walls, and taking fruit from gardens or orchards is simply stealing. In some parts of France there are local laws about taking chestnuts, mushrooms (and snails), because these are cash crops. Signs like *Réserve de Chasse*, or *Chasse Privé* indicate that the shooting is reserved for the landowner. As a general rule, behave sensibly and you will be tolerated everywhere, even on private land.

The country code

Walkers in France should obey the *Code du Randonneur*:

● Love and respect Nature.
● Avoid unnecessary noise.
● Destroy nothing.
● Do not leave litter.
● Do not pick flowers or plants.
● Do not disturb wildlife.
● Re-close all gates.
● Protect and preserve the habitat.
● No smoking or fires in the forests. (This rule is essential and is actively enforced by foresters and police.)
● Stay on the footpath.
● Respect and understand the country way of life and the country people.
● Think of others as you think of yourself.

Transport

Transportation to and within France is generally excellent. There are no less than nine Channel ports: Dunkirk, Calais, Boulogne, Dieppe, Le Havre, Caen/Ouistreham, Cherbourg, Saint-Malo and Roscoff, and a surprising number of airports served by direct flights from the UK. Although some of the services are seasonal, it is often possible to fly direct to Toulouse, Poitiers, Nantes, Perpignan, Montpellier, indeed to many provincial cities, as well as to Paris and such obvious destinations as Lyon and Nice. Within France the national railway, the SNCF, still retains a nationwide network. Information, tickets and a map can be obtained from the SNCF. France also has a good country bus service and the *gare routière* is often placed just beside the railway station. Be aware though, that many French bus services only operate within the *département*, and they do not generally operate from one provincial city to the next. I cannot encourage people to hitch-hike, which is both illegal and risky, but walkers might consider a taxi for their luggage. Almost every French village has a taxi driver who will happily transport your rucksacks to the next night-stop, fifteen to twenty miles away, for Fr.50 a head or even less.

Money

Walking in France is cheap, but banks are not common in the smaller villages, so carry a certain amount of French money and the rest in traveller's cheques or Eurocheques, which are accepted everywhere.

Clothing and equipment

The amount of clothing and equipment you will need depends on the terrain, the length of the walk, the time of your visit, the accommodation used. Outside the mountain areas it is not necessary to take the full range of camping or backpacking gear. I once walked across France from the Channel to the Camargue along the Grande Randonnée footpaths in March, April and early May and never needed to use any of the camping gear I carried in my rucksack because I found hotels everywhere, even in quite small villages.

Essential items are:
In summer: light boots, a hat, shorts, suncream, lip salve, mosquito repellent, sunglasses, a sweater, a windproof cagoule, a small first-aid kit, a walking stick.
In winter: a change of clothing, stormproof outer garments, gaiters, hat, lip salve, a companion.
In the mountains at any time: large-scale maps (1:25,000), a compass, an ice-axe. In winter, add a companion and ten-point crampons.
At any time: a phrase book, suitable maps, a dictionary, a sense of humour.

The best guide to what to take lies in the likely weather and the terrain. France tends to be informal, so there is no need to carry a jacket or something smart for the evenings. I swear by Rohan clothing, which is light, smart and functional. The three things I would never go without are light, well-broken-in boots and several pairs of loop-stitched socks, and my walking stick.

Health hazards
Health hazards are few. France can be hot in summer, so take a full water-bottle and refill it at every opportunity. A small first-aid kit is sensible, with plasters and 'mole-skin' for blisters, but since prevention is better than cure, loop-stitched socks and flexible boots are better. Any French chemist — a *pharmacie* — is obliged to render first-aid treatment for a small fee. These pharmacies can be found in most villages and large towns and are marked by a green cross.

Dogs are both a nuisance and a hazard. All walkers in France should carry a walking stick to fend off aggressive curs. Rabies — *la rage* — is endemic and anyone bitten must seek immediate medical advice. France also possesses two types of viper, which are common in the hill areas of the south. In fairness, although I found my walking stick indispensable, I must add that in thirty years I have never even seen a snake or a rabid dog. In case of real difficulty, dial 17 for the police and the ambulance.

Food and wine
One of the great advantages with walking in France is that you can end the day with a good meal and not gain an ounce. French country cooking is generally excellent and good value for money, with the price of a four-course menu starting at about Fr.45. The ingredients for the mid-day picnic can be purchased from the village shops and these also sell wine. Camping-Gaz cylinders and cartridges are widely available, as is 2-star petrol for stoves. Avoid naked fires.

Preparation
The secret of a good walk lies in making adequate preparations before you set out. It pays to be fit enough to do the daily distance at the start. Much of the necessary information is contained in this guide, but if you need more, look in guidebooks or outdoor magazines, or ask friends.

The French
I cannot close this introduction without saying a few words about the French, not least because the walker in France is going to meet rather more French people than, say, a motorist will, and may even meet French people who have never met a foreigner before. It does help if the visitor speaks a little French, even if only enough to say '*bonjour*' and '*Merci*' and '*S'il vous plaît*'. The French tend to be formal and it pays to be

polite, to say 'hello', to shake hands. I am well aware that relations between France and England have not always been cordial over the last six hundred years or so, but I have never met with hostility of any kind in thirty years of walking through France. Indeed, I have always found that if the visitor is prepared to meet the French halfway, they will come more than halfway to greet him or her in return, and are both friendly and hospitable to the passing stranger.

As a final tip, try smiling. Even in France, or especially in France, a smile and a *'pouvez vous m'aider?'* (Can you help me?) will work wonders. That's my last bit of advice, and all I need do now is wish you *'Bonne Route'* and good walking in France.

WALKS IN PROVENCE

Robin Neillands

Provence is the romantic, historic province of Southern France: historic because this is the old Roman colony, the *Provincia Romana*, hence the name Provence, and romantic because it is beautiful, a place for lovers as well as walkers, a countryside of wine and gaiety, rich with the scents of wild flowers and lavender, studded with little hill-towns and villages. The walker would have to be very short on soul not to find Provence delightful, and as for Roman remains, these are everywhere, at Arles and Orange, along the coast, in the hills behind Nice, wherever your feet will take you.

Today, of course, Provence is a popular holiday area and full of second homes for people from all over Europe, who have descended on the hills of the Var and Vaucluse to convert the old Provençal *mas* into holiday villas.

Much of Provence is the back-country, the *arrière-pays* to the famous Côte d'Azur, the Riviera, but it is still surprising that just a few kilometres from the coast, the hinterland of Provence becomes quite empty of people, even remote. Most of the modern development has been along the coast, but most of the older towns stand on hilltops a little inland, beyond easy reach of the old Barbary Corsairs, and the more garish modern accretions are easily avoided. This is good walking country, a place for serious walkers.

Walkers who come south to walk in the hills of Provence will find them rugged, and in summer anyway, extremely hot. Boots, trousers against the thorns, and plenty of water are going to be essential, but any little local difficulty is going to be more than compensated for by the glorious scenery and the marvellous weather. The walks in this book have been carefully chosen to present every facet of this province, from the yawning Canyon du Verdon in the north, to the beautiful *calanques*, the deep bays along the coast, south of Aubagne — which is the modern home of the Foreign Legion, incidentally. Backpackers will certainly enjoy the long trip from Sisteron on the River Durance across the mountains and the Plateau de Vaucluse to the fortress town of Tarascon on the Rhône, passing through the Daudet country, but the entire province is so full of good walks of every kind that there is something here for every kind of walker. Provence is especially interesting to those who love botany, wildlife and the quiet out-of-the-way places where the other tourists don't go, as well as just outright walking.

Getting there

Getting to the area is quite easy, although it lies a good six hundred miles from the nearest Channel ports. There are motorway connections via Lyon and Paris, excellent and very fast TGV trains from Paris, and two airports at Nice and Marseilles, each with frequent flights from London. Within the province there are plenty of train connections into the hinterland up the river valleys from Aix-en-Provence to Sisteron and Digne, all along the coast from Nice and up the Rhône Valley and, most usefully, into the *arrière pays* north of Nice on the *Chemin de Fer de Provence*, a small line that begins in Nice and rattles around the hills through Entrevaux to Digne. Many of these station halts are stopping points for local buses. The buses are not frequent, and operate on a departmental basis, but they can be found at the *gare routière* in Nice, Aix, Marseilles and Toulon, the most likely points of departure on arrival in Provence.

Accommodation

In the hinterland, the accommodation can be rather limited, although even the smallest village will usually have one hotel or rooms over the cafe. Generally speaking, the nearer the coast, the more widely available the accommodation, and those who go deep into the hills or across the Vaucluse may need to take a tent. *Gîtes d'Étape* are fairly common and more are being built all the time, but except in the higher hills, where a tent is a sensible precaution anyway, the walker should have no difficulty finding accommodation. There are plenty of camp sites, and wild camping is always possible over the 800 metre mark.

Climate

This is the Mediterranean and though generally mild, with the mimosa in flower by February, the climate tends to be extreme. There will be snow on the hilltops of the Vaucluse, Var and Luberon hills from late November even into May, but the weather will always be changeable. I recall setting off one January in shirtsleeves from Sisteron and waking up next morning to a howling blizzard. In the summer months, June to September, it can be very hot and so walkers will probably choose to travel in the Spring or Autumn months, when the temperatures are lower. Depending on the season and terrain, water-bottles and ice-axes may be essential.

Terrain

The Provençal terrain is very varied but rarely easy. This is a region of *maquis*, scrub, gorse, lavender, high meadows, vines, and a great deal of loose rock. The hills go up to the 1000m (300 ft) mark or perhaps a little higher, which is not too high, but they tend to go up quite steeply. These are not gentle ridges but real rugged mountains, not to be taken lightly. Mont Ventoux, north of the Vaucluse plateau, is a real mountain by any standard at 1909m (6200 ft), and do not be fooled by the fact that a road runs over the top, the weather on Ventoux can be very wild indeed. Provence is a very beautiful part of France, but the terrain is rugged and remote. You can easily go all day without seeing a soul, and must therefore take sensible precautions — like a good map, a compass and, if possible, a companion.

Clothing and equipment

As in all mountain areas, the weather can be changeable and never more so than here, where the Alps lie just to the north, the Mediterranean just to the south and the *mistral*-swept funnel of the Rhône Valley lies to the west. As a general guide, dress and equip yourself for extremes of heat or cold and in the 'tween seasons of Spring and Autumn, be prepared for sudden changes — take shorts *and* an extra sweater, and if going anywhere high, carry an ice-axe. It can be quite remarkably chilly early in the morning at height in Provence, so be careful of ice on rock or when crossing streams. A good mosquito repellent with a high 'deet' factor would not go amiss in high summer, and two water-bottles will certainly be necessary in the hotter months.

Hazards

There are said to be vipers in the hills of Provence, but I have never seen one. The main hazards will be thirst and a shortage of water in summer, and cold high winds in winter, with snow on the tops until May in normal years. A stick to fend off farmyard curs and shepherd's dogs would also be useful.

Food and drink

The Côte d'Azur has more good restaurants than anywhere else in France outside Paris, and Provence has produced some noted chefs. In the hills the food tends to be tasty and ample, rather than *raffiné*, but good value for money, with most of the smaller village restaurants offering menus for Fr.45. There is an abundance of good wine, including local vintages from the Luberon and Ventoux and excellent red wines from the Cotes du Rhone. Walkers will eat very well at no great cost in the smaller villages. Dishes to look out for are *bouillabaisse* (fish soup), which you will find well inland, and *estouffe* and *daube*, local stews full of garlic. The fruit and cheese are excellent. Any dish *à la Provencale* will contain tomatoes, garlic, olive oil, herbs and onions.

Where to go walking

The walks in this guide offer a very wide assortment of walking, so the choice is yours. Backpackers will certainly enjoy the Sisteron to Tarascon walk, on the GR6, and the Gorges du Verdon walk, although not long is very different, very exciting and definitely worth ranking as one of the world's great walks. For something equally enjoyable but shorter, and perhaps suitable for those who do not want to backpack, the Saint Pilon–Calanques on the GR98 is a good suggestion, marvellous walking with ever more frequent glimpses of the sea.

Back on the long-distance walking or backpacking route, the trip along the GR4 from Grasse to Manosque is a beautiful walk, with the old town of Castellane and the gorge of Verdon along the way. There is good day walking from all these places, and since Grasse is the perfume centre of France, the terrain around there is greener and grassier than in the hills to the north or south.

A good centre for walking in Provence is Pont-de-Mirabeau on the GR9. This guide suggests walks in either direction, south to Ste Baume or north to Brantes. Parts of the GR6 to Tarascon, overlap with the northern part of the Tour du Luberon footpath. The Luberon hills are well worth exploring, and a walk along the northern crest would be a delightful hill walk, as would any of the walks from St Pilon, a 944m (3260 ft) peak in the Massif de Ste Baume. This area is well forested and mercifully shady, even in the heat of summer, and said to be the place where Saint Mary Magdalene lived after she landed at Saintes Maries-de-la-Mer, on the edge of the Camargue in AD43.

The walking in Provence is quite different from anything the walker will have experienced in England, largely because the climate and terrain is completely Mediterranean. Those who like sunshine and vast views will find Provencal walking among the finest in the world, but do avoid the hot months of July and August — down in the south of France, it can get very hot indeed.

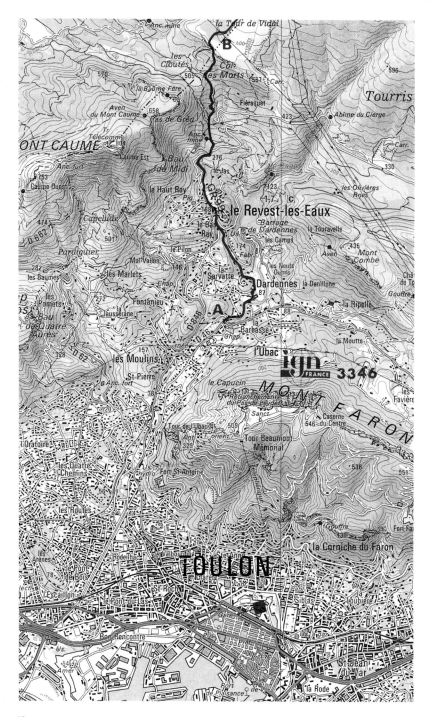

WALK 1

TOOLON
🏛 ⛺ ✕ 🚂 🚌
🚎 🛈

Toulon is an old city, rich in military and maritime history; it is the chief naval port in France, but also a port for pleasure craft, boasting the most beautiful natural harbour in Europe. There are numerous forts and towers constructed by de Vauban, the great French military engineer, which used to encircle the town. At the top of Mont Faron, the Beaumont Tower houses the memorial to the Allied landings in Provence in August 1944. You can reach it on foot, by cable-car or by road. Musée de la Marine (Marine Museum), at the Arsenal Gate; the Musée du Vieux Toulon (Museum of Old Toulon); the municipal museum, which houses the natural history museum, the museum of art and archaeology, a photography room and library.

0:35

The walk begins at the northern edge of Toulon, in the suburb of Dardennes, on route D46 (marked A on the map). To get there, starting from Toulon station, take the Avenue Vauban as far as Boulevard Leclerc-de-Hautecloque, then turn left to reach the Place de la Liberté, where you take the bus to Dardennes. Get off at Pont de Dardennes. The GR99 crosses the bridge to enter Dardennes (where you will find a bakery and a grocery) and follows the D46, but then leaves it for a path climbing up on the right; this then meets the Val-d'Ardène road, which you take as far as Le Revest-les-Eaux.

LE REVEST-LES-EAUX
🚂 ✕ 🚌

Last place to stock up on water until Signes. 17th century castle; 17th century church built by the Carthusian monks of Montrieux, with a good view over the village from the tall square belfry tower.

1:30

The path runs in front of the *mairie* of Le Revest along the Boulevard d'Estienne-d'Orves and turns into the Chemin du Stade. At the point where it curves left, go straight ahead (north) on the stony pathway that rises to meet the road to the quarry. Take the right-hand fork, then follow the road on your left, which is signposted for the Stade de la colline. Keep climbing the winding path as far as the Col des Morts.

Col des Morts
490m; view over Toulon, the harbour and surroundings. The chalky zone around Siou Blanc is honeycombed with

From the Col des Morts, the path continues north-east across a dry plain. At the cross-roads (see map IGN ref. 668), do not take the right-hand road marked out in blue, which leads to the Grand Cam. Take the path which

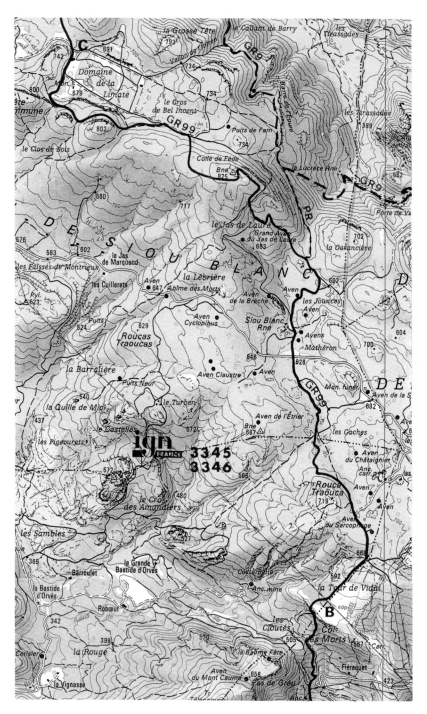

potholes (avens), characteristic of the karstic (rough limestone) area.

runs in a generally north-west direction, passing the foot of Rouca Traouca, and join the forest route (see map IGN ref 628), which leads to the restored farm of Siou Blanc (this provides shelter, but is indicated as a ruin on the map). The GR99 comes to a crossroads at Les Jounces (602 metres), where it bears left (north-west). In the vicinity of Garancière, you will find a PR path.

1:40

Sentier PR

620m; marked out in green, it leaves GR99 on the right to link up with GR9.

The GR99 carries on to cross a section of the Siou Blanc plateau. Climb a steep, rocky incline to reach a cliff; walk along its edge until you reach a cairn which is marked 'Mire de la Limate' with a painted arrow; this indicates the direction. The area is called the Colle de Fede. Go left to reach a ledge where there is a geodesic sign. With that behind you, make for the spot marked on the ground in blue and green, from which the path extends up the ridge road, then descends to a wide road bordered by a fence/hedge.

Domaine de la Limate

700m; a vast, chalky plateau surrounded by rocky ridges.

Take the left-hand path; a little further on, turn left to skirt the Limate plain and the farm of the same name. After the farm, follow the road (which is also used by cars). At the bend marked C on the map, leave the left-hand road and go straight ahead (north, then north-west). You descend to the plain by a winding track. Cross a stream, the Latay, by the footbridge, and walk along by the cemetery. A little further on you will meet the GR9, which to the right (east) would take you to Saint-Pons-les-Mûres. Both paths run into Signes together.

1:20

SIGNES

⌂ 🏕 🚂 🚌

340m; a district of Signes, a largely wooded area. It is an excellent place to stay and a good departure point for a number of walks. Since the 12th century, the feast of Saint Jean and Saint Eloi has been celebrated on 23 June with processions, floats and fireworks. At the chapel of Saint-Jean they make an offering of lemons. Castellas from the Ligurian era (c.600 BC); ancient

After the church, the GR99 leaves the GR9, which continues east (see p. 00) and north to the Pont de Mirabeau. At the last house in Signes, the GR99 runs north along the Promenades campsite, then skirts a washing place. Via the Rue de Briançon, it joins a road turning left; at the fork further on, go right (north-east) up a stony path to Gaude. After that you climb east, then north, following a path with cartwheel tracks on each side. You will find a track to follow on the right; 500 metres on, at the crossroads, take a right between the bushes to reach Verguine farm.

0:45

walls; Gallo-Roman site; clock tower in the marketplace; church of Saint-Pierre, with 15th century doorway; 15th/16th century chapel of Saint-Jean; chapel of Saint-Clair, with plaque commemorating the Austro-Sardinian defeat in 1709.

Ferme de la Verguine
744m.

1:15

The path crosses the Agnis plain in a north-easterly direction, again becomes a track, then swerves left to reach Agnis farm, with its ancient stone threshing floor and wells. Pass this farm on the right, and climb up a steep footpath to a desert-like plateau to reach the edge of the Petite Colle.

Petite Colle
902m; a large rock, from which you can see Sainte-Baume, Sainte-Victoire, Lure mountain, the Alps and Saint-Maximin plain.

Detour *1 hr*
by PR to
Col Notre Dame
747m.

Detour, see left. Follow the left-hand PR footpath marked in yellow (it is also marked on the map) via the Mourré d'Agnis. At the pass, the junction with GR9, there is a ruined oratory.

1:30

Skirting the large rocks on the right, known as *baous*, the GR99 follows the line of the ridge to the north-east. In parts it goes along the cliff edge, so be especially careful in foggy weather. Pass by a geodesic sign (852m). At the Pic de Caucadis, the path leaves the cliff and descends to the forest as far as the Col de Caucadis, then goes along a track and veers left (north-east, then north) as it descends to a valley. You will pass the ruins of a château and come out in the village square at Mazaugues.

MAZAUGUES
🏠 ✕ ⚓
410m; although Mazaugues means 'the land of water', the boring of the Provence canal in the massif has dried up most of the springs.

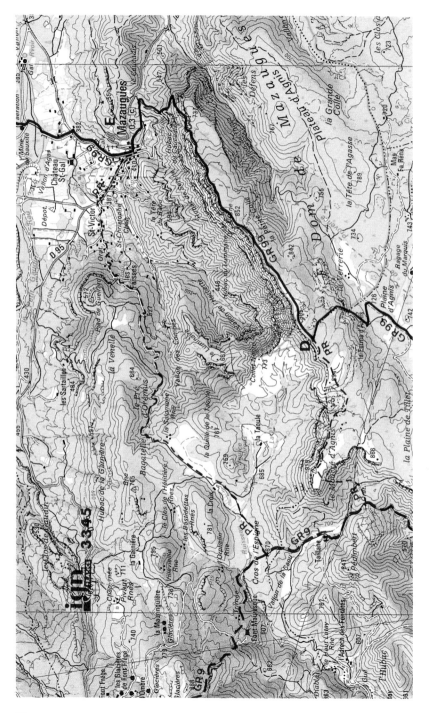

Detour *2 hrs 30 mins by PR to*
Cros de l'Espigne
670m
junction with the GR9.

1

Detour, see left. Follow the PR path, which is marked in yellow, westwards via Saint-Victor and the Pré d'Orémus. From the Cros de l'Espigne it is possible to return to Mazaugues by following the GR9 southwards, then the PR path left at the ruined oratory as far as the Petite Colle (point D on the map), finally returning to Mazaugues via the GR99. This circular walk takes 5 hours from leaving Mazaugues.

The GR99 passes the church in Mazaugues and takes the road D95 northwards. After the cemetery, at the crossroads (see map IGN ref 382), leave this route for a road on your left. Further on, take the left-hand road for a few metres and, near a ventilation shaft, take the right-hand path that goes down a gully, then cross the stream at the ford. The path goes directly north along the stone slabs of the Caire de Sarrazin. Trace a wide arc round a wooded hilltop, the Claou de la Chevalière, and you will arrive at the ruins of Ambard.

Ruines d'Ambard
357m

Detour *45 mins*
TOURVES 🏠 🚉 🚌 🛈
287m

Detour, see left. Go to the left along the PR footpath, marked first in yellow and green, then just in yellow.

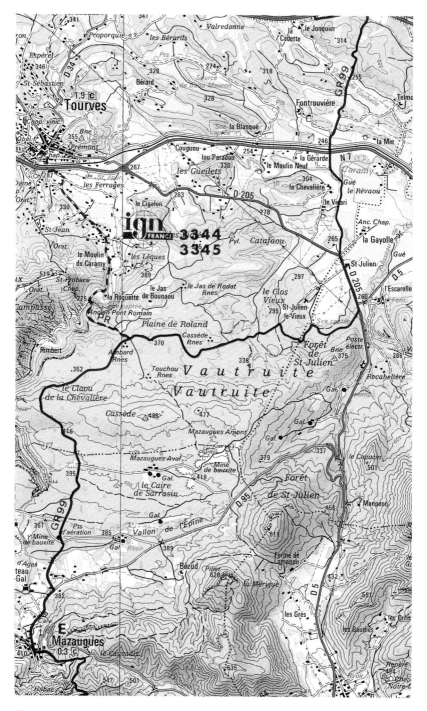

0:20

The path winds round towards the east, passing near the ruins of the Cassède farm. Further on, where several roads intersect, don't go straight on towards Saint-Julien-le-Vieux, but turn right and walk until you come to the crossroads of the D5 and D205. Here, take the D205 left as far as the Château de Saint-Julien.

**CHÂTEAU DE
SAINT-JULIEN**
◻ **Å**
250m
agricultural land.

2:30

Shortly after passing the château, leave the D205 and turn right, then left (north) on the road which crosses the plain, descending to the banks of the River Caramy. Cross this stream by the rudimentary bridge made from two tree trunks. Continue left through a field as far as route N7.

ROUTE N7
Ⓗ 🚌
246m

1:30

The route crosses the main road, then a railway and continues northwards by a path as far as the A8 motorway. Near Jonquier, go underneath the motorway. The path first turns right (east), then left along a metalled road climbing to the Cros de la Putan woods. Via the valley slope and across the vineyards, in a north-north-west direction, you will come to Bras.

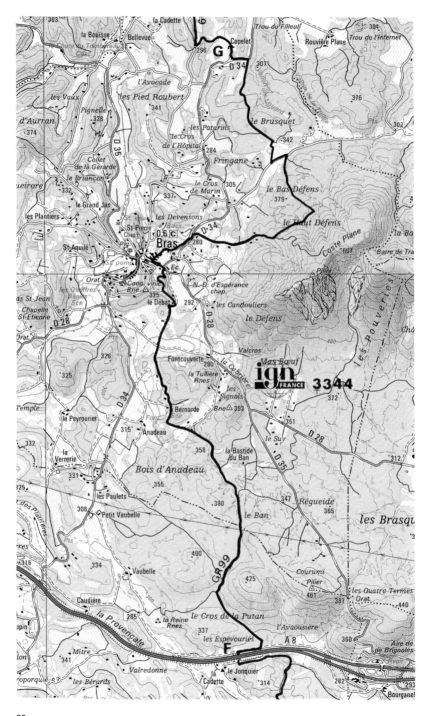

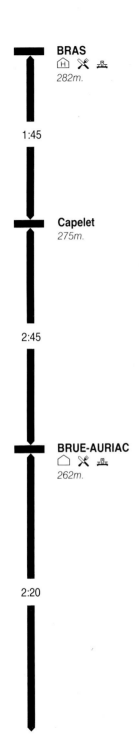

BRAS
282m.

1:45

Capelet
275m.

2:45

BRUE-AURIAC
262m.

2:20

The route passes a mission cross and the war memorial, skirts the school and follows the D34 towards the north-east. Before you reach a little bridge (see map IGN ref 280), take the road on your right which climbs eastward in the woods to a sort of pass, then goes down through the area of Bas Défens until it reaches a road. Turn left at the road, then turn right (north) on to the road which goes round the ruins of Vieux Brusquet. When you come to the road D34, turn left for a few metres, then take a right towards the farm (*mas*) at Capelet.

From the mas de Capelet, the path goes east and meets a road at IGN map ref 296. Turn right and go north along this road for a short distance, but instead of following it when it turns right, continue in the same direction on a smaller road which borders the Ponton hill. This road descends to cross the River Argens at the Pont de Saint-Saumian, an arched stone bridge. The River Argens tumbles into a gorge here. After the bridge, the path turns left along the course of the Argens, skirts a vineyard, then takes a track north, up through the woods. In the woods, it passes the 11th century chapel of Notre-Dame, after which it descends to the road (D560). Follow the road to the right as far as Brue-Auriac.

In front of the church, the route curves left towards the west and follows a road. After 2 kilometres, at the bend of the road, leave the road for a path that mounts the valley of Piégros. With the Bastide de Piégros on your right, cross the Camp d'Aigues-Mortes plateau in a northerly direction. In the area of Rimade (marked H on the map), turn north-west towards the ruined sheepfold of Roussoni. From there you climb up as far as the Bastide de Valensole. Do not stop there, as it is private property. Ignore the surfaced road and take the rocky path on your right, which leads to the park of the Château de Saint-Martin. At the furthest edge of the château wall, the GR99 turns right and enters Saint-Martin-des-Pallières. On the left you will find the beginning of the separate route GR99a, which joins up with route GR9 at La Neuve farm on the D11, near the Mirabeau bridge.

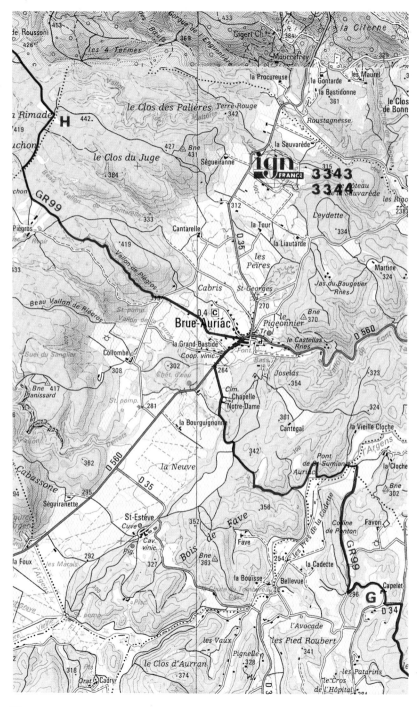

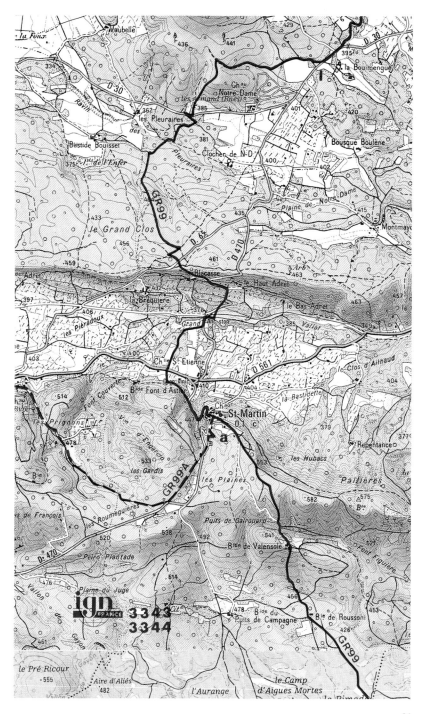

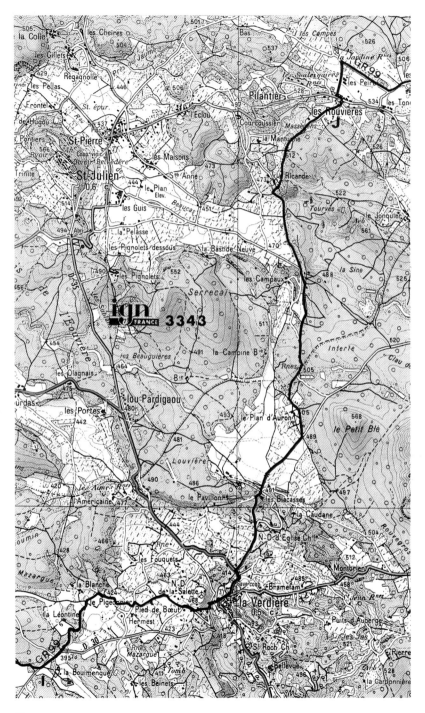

Saint-Martin-des-Pallières
500m
No provisions available here, but you can go to Esparron, 5 km west on the GR99a.

1

La Bouimengue
390m
Point I on the map.

1:45

LA VERDIÈRE
Å ✕ ⚓
450m

2

Les Rouvières
542m

Detour *1 hr 15 mins*
SAINT-PIERRE
Å ⚓

The GR99 descends northwards by a little street and then a footpath. Follow the D470 for 300 metres, then, at a wayside cross, take the left-hand path which leads to the Bastide du Font d'Astier. Leaving this path behind you to your left, cut across the D561 and continue straight ahead (north), cross a stream, the Grand Vallat, and you will arrive at the old Saint-Martin station. Go right, along the old railway line, then continue along the D470 and its shortcuts. At a sharp bend in the road, take the path on your left (west), which leads to the farm at La Blacasse. North of Blacasse farm, turn right (north-west), cutting across the D65. Continue in that direction, then northwards, descending the valley of Les Fleuraies. Cross the D30 to reach the ruined farm of Les Armand. The footpath rises to the north, and then east, skirting the Notre-Dame estate and arriving at the D30 at the level of La Bouimengue.

Turn left along the D30, leaving it after 500 metres at a bend, and continue opposite (north-east) as far as the farm of Le Pigeonnier, which might provide shelter. The GR continues east by road — you will come across a spring at a corner — and then by a path to reach La Verdière.

The route reaches a crossroads with the D554, passes the wine co-operative, the cemetery and the campsite, then shortly afterwards (see map IGN ref 414) goes right along a road, ascending in the direction of Les Blacasses. From Les Blacasses, the road continues until you reach the crossroads (see map IGN ref 489), where you take the dirt path left (north) leading to Le Plan d'Auron. Continue past a ruined sheepfold (505m), then further on, you pass near the farm of Les Campeaux. Continuing north on the pathway, you reach the *mas* (farm) de la Ricarde. The GR99 then twists north-east to reach Les Rouvières.

Detour, see left. Go eastwards along route D69. Near Saint-Pierre, at Saint-Julien-le-Montagné, is a Romanesque church and 13th century ramparts.

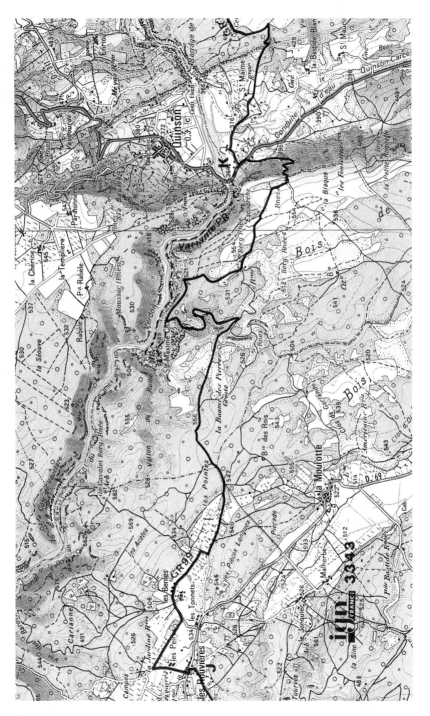

The GR99 passes in front of the church at Rouvières, takes the D69 on the left and when it reaches an oratory, goes towards Les Peires. Further on, turn right (south-east) to pass the hamlet of Les Bernes, then the area of Les Pointes. At the fork in the path (IGN map ref 556), ignore the right-hand track for riders (marked in orange), which leads to La Baume des Pierres, a cave which sheltered Resistance fighters in 1944. The GR99 goes straight ahead towards the east, goes down into a valley which you follow northwards, then goes up a steep slope as far as the road to La Chapelle.

Chemin de la Chapelle
Detour *15 mins*
along PR footpath to
Chapelle Sainte-Maxime
489m
built in 1854; a curious ancient fortified tower nearby.

On the left, there is a PR footpath marked in yellow.

Alternative route from Chemin de la Chapelle to the canal bridge. This route takes an hour and is marked in dashes on the map. It is only suitable for people who are well-prepared and fit. From the chapel, you follow the difficult track marked out in yellow which descends to the old Verdon canal.

The GR99 passes the PR and goes west. It turns right and passes the remains of a brick oratory at 521 metres, then leads southwards past some sheepfolds. Once through a little pass, you descend left (north) by a winding path to route D13 and the bridge over the Verdon canal.

1:45

Vieux canal du Verdon
(Old Verdon canal) 375m.
Detour *20 mins*
north along the D13 to
QUINSON
Ⓗ ⚓
372m

3

The GR99 follows the road D13 to the left for 100 metres. Near the big bridge over the Verdon (IGN map ref 364), the yellow difficult route from the Sainte-Maxime chapel (marked in dashes on the map), rejoins the GR99, which then leaves the road for the path on the right. This leads to a beach with a campsite. It crosses a bridge over the Verdon canal and climbs south-west up to the plateau. It first turns north, then east, passes the fountain at Les Aumades, descends north-east to a valley then rises again to Artignosc-sur-Verdon.

ARTIGNOSC-SUR-VERDON
⚓
504m
Water at the fountain.

The GR99 turns left in front of the co-operative at Artignosc, goes along by the cemetery and passes beside the chapel of Notre-Dame. It then descends to the Grignolets valley, skirts a knoll on which sits the restored farm of

Barbatelle, and rises north-east by a path which reaches Baudinard.

Detour *30 mins*
L'AVELANÈDE
⌂ ⚑

Walk south-east along a path marked in yellow.

BAUDINARD
🏨 ⌂

The inn (four rooms) is not open in summer. 630m; the PR path from Artignosc (marked in dashes on the map) rejoins the GR here, as does another which provides a circular walk via l'Arbitelle.

Château des Sabran-Baudinard

A juicy Provencal anecdote is attached to the ruins of the Château des Sabran-Baudinard. It was collected by L. Henseling, who related it in his book Zigzags in the Var *(1932):*
'During the internecine wars that devastated Provence, the people of Baudinard were taken by surprise one day by neighbouring enemies, who were superior in number. The people were already talking about surrender when the local lord had an idea for a cunning trick.
When the enemy was preparing for assault at first light, he told the women, children and old men – in short, all those who couldn't carry arms – to go up on the ramparts and to reveal themselves at the arrow-slits in the battlements . . . with their buttocks towards the assailants. When the latter arrived beneath the walls of the château, they recoiled

Alternative route from Artignosc to Baudinard. Follow the PR path (marked in yellow) northwards, passing the farm at l'Arbitelle; the way is marked in dashes on the map.

The GR follows the Grand'Rue and, when it comes up to the town hall, near the washing fountain, goes up the steps that lead beyond the cluster of buildings. A little further on, on the right, is a curious tower on a pyramid base: this is the keep of the old Château des Sabran-Baudinard. Go along by the bowls ground and climb up towards a wayside cross.

The GR rises in a south-easterly direction along a path which follows the ridge, and provides a view to the left over the lake of Sainte-Croix to the Alps of Haute-Provence, and to the right of the hills of the mid-Var. You pass near a barn and sheepfold. Then a little further on the GR turns sharp left (north-west) on to a track through a small valley, then bends north-east and descends to Sainte-Croix lake. Take the D49 right, and cross a dyke-bridge to reach the crossroads, where you take route D71 left as far as the outskirts of Bauduen.

2

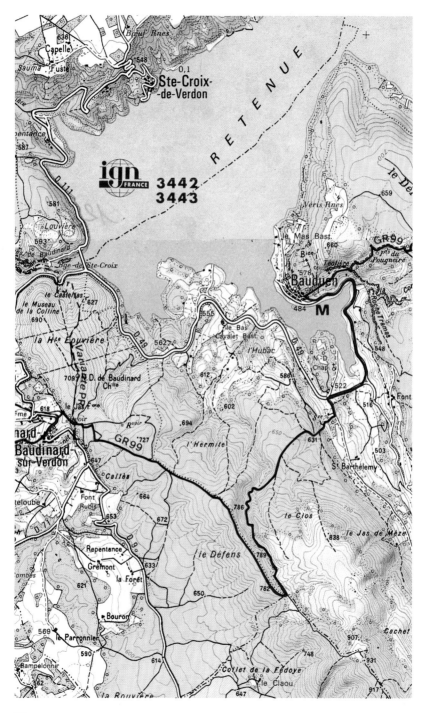

*from the — er — faces of the
defendants, then there was
an uproar and they fled
away, shouting that the place
was defended by . . . the
Cyclops.'*

BAUDUEN
🏠 ▲ ⛵

*484m; artificial lake of
Sainte-Croix (area of 2500
hectares) containing millions
of cubic metres, which
enables the production of
162 kilowatts of electricity
per annum. The lake extends
to the foot of the village, and
has contributed to its
development as a tourist
centre.*

0:30

Just before entering Bauduen, the GR takes
the road north-east (right) then a path climbing
up to the Défens plateau. At a bend, leave this
path which goes on to the south-east, and
continue north-east by a path which enters a
small valley and passes under a cable. Further
on, you will emerge on to a bend in route
D957, not far from a house, the Bastide de la
Pérassée.

Bastide de la Pérassée
529m
Detour *45 mins
north along route D957 to*
LES
SALLES-SUR-VERDON
🏠 ▲ ✕ ⛵

*This village was entirely
reconstructed in 1974 to
replace the one formerly
situated in the Verdon valley
which was inundated by the
creation of Lake
Sainte-Croix.*

1

The GR follows the road for 400 metres, then
climbs up to the right by a twisting parth to the
Château de Chanteraine.

CHANTERAINE
🏠 ✕

*600m
(Point N on the map)*

The route continues up the old Chemin (path)
d'Aiguines, rising towards the north-east, goes
along route D19, then approaches the
Château d'Aiguines.

Château d'Aiguines
*Built in the sixteenth century.
It is a massive, four-square
structure, with four pepper-
pot towers covered in
glazed, multi-coloured tiles.*

You then climb up to the village of Aiguines.

AIGUINES
🏠 ✕ ⛵

*800m. Tourist centre close
to the gorges of Verdon. The*

Warning: Be sure to stock up with sufficient
water and food here, as there is nowhere to
obtain them amidst the ridges and gorges of
Verdon.

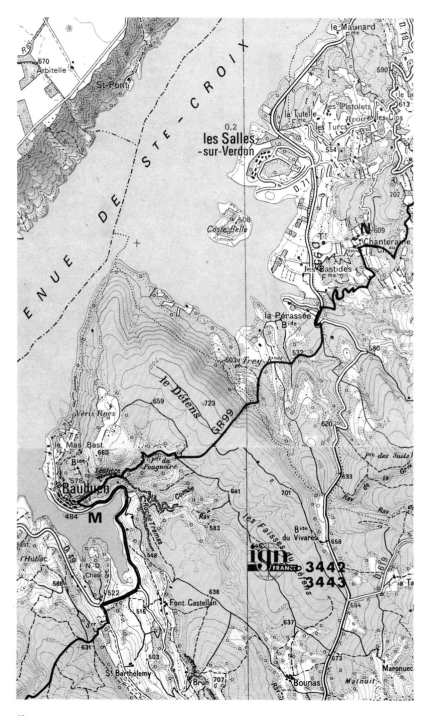

village is famous for its production of boxwood objects and the studded boules used in the Provençal game and has a museum of wood-turning.

The GR passes the post office and goes up to the chapel of Saint-Pierre, at which point there is a panoramic view over Lake Sainte-Croix and the plateau of Valensole. Walk along by the remains of the feudal château, and then by a reservoir. From this point, as far as the Petite Fôret (Little Forest), the itinerary of the GR99 via the Grand Margès can be tricky to negotiate in bad weather. To avoid it, take the alternative route described below, which branches off on the left near IGN map ref 1094.

This route is marked out in yellow, and goes via the Col d'Iloire; taking about 2½ hours. It is marked by dashes on the map. It has some tricky stretches amidst the rocks and scree.

After the reservoir, the GR99 crosses the main road D71 (the 'Corniche sublime' route) to climb a very steep path as far as the area of Le Puits.

Le Puits
1094m

Warning: if the weather is bad, it is safer to leave the GR here, and to take the path marked on the left (north), which descends to the Col d'Iloire, where you can follow the alternative path described below: see the dashes on the map.

Alternative route from Le Puits to La Petite Fôret. From Le Puits, the GR99 takes a south-easterly direction, skirts the edge of the rocky ridge, and rises to a pass at 1432 metres, the Col de Faou de Chabrot.

1

Col de Faou de Chabrot
1432m
Detour 20 mins
Source de Vaumale
1:30
Descend northwards by the path marked in yellow, to this spring which provides the water supply to Aiguines.

Go round a mound, which used to arch over a glacier. At the turn of the century, people brought bottles and containers here to freeze them for the use of sick people. The GR crosses a field, winds among the rocky ridges, and along a high crest mounts to the Signal du Grand-Margès.

Signal du Grand-Margès
1577m
There is a panorama over the entire region of the Var, as far as the sea and the Alps of Haute-Provence, with an extraordinary view
1:15
over the gorges of Verdon.

The GR more or less clings to the rocky ridge, then goes down a grassy slope. We recommend that you do not wander off on to the paths which go down to the right to the army camp at Canjuers, as firing and manoeuvres may be taking place. At the end of the pass, turn left (north) on a path that goes down through a beech forest. You can see the

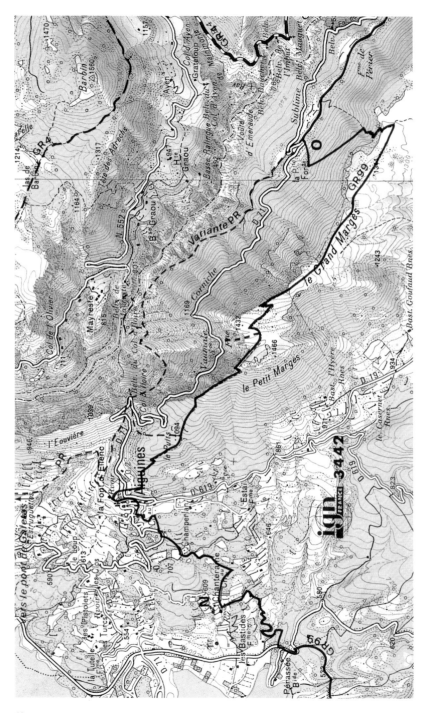

remains of the cabins where the craftspeople from Aiguines used to work the wood they had collected. The path zigzags to a bend in the D71 in the vicinity of La Petite Forêt.

La Petite Forêt

970m

the arrival point of the alternative path that comes via the Col d'Iloire (see the dashes on the map). **Note**: *it is this itinerary that walkers coming from the other direction must follow in bad weather in order to avoid the Grand Margès.*

The GR turns right (south-east) along a dirt path as far as the Fontaine de Périer, then goes left along a path which descends to the D71. Go right along the D71, then after 100 metres leave it for the Auberge des Cavaliers on the left.

AUBERGE DES CAVALIERS

⌂ ✗

780m

see P on the map. Open only in the season; there is nowhere to get water.

Warning: at the Auberge des Cavaliers, the GR99 joins up with the GR4 and descends to the Grand Canyon of Verdon. This route should only be taken by people who are fit, used to real trekking, not subject to vertigo, and who are properly shod.

● You should only undertake this route in good weather.
● Beware of rock slides near the cliffs.
● Avoid the metal ladders in a thunderstorm.
● Take a good torch for the tunnels.
● First-aid posts: see the list of useful addresses.

The GR99 bypasses the Auberge des Cavaliers, crosses the Pas des Cavaliers and descends by some steps cut into the rock, then by a ladder, lastly by a twisting path to Verdon. Cross the river on the footbridge, go under the telegraph wire and climb up as far as the junction with the GR4.

Junction with the GR4.

Near Q on the map.

Alternative route from Auberge des Cavaliers to Chalet du Point Sublime, avoiding the Gorges de Verdon.

Take the path marked in yellow eastwards; it goes via the Etroit des Cavaliers, the bridge at l'Artuby, Le Petit Saint-Maymes (see R on the map), the farm at Entreverges and the bridge at Tusset. This route is marked out in dashes on the map and takes about 5 hours.

Important: Walkers are urged not to take — or create — short-cuts through the uneven,

43

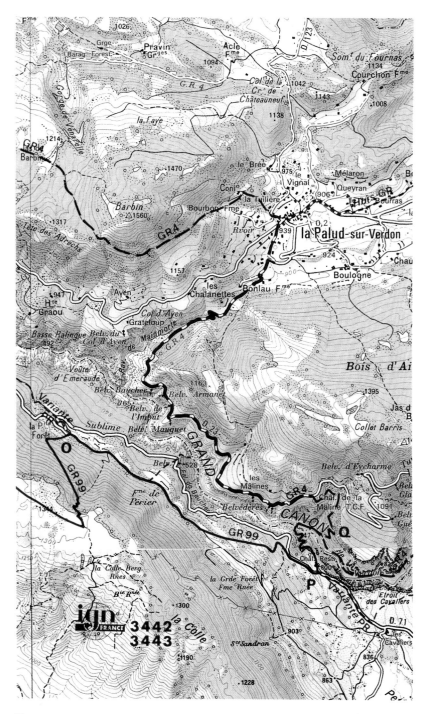

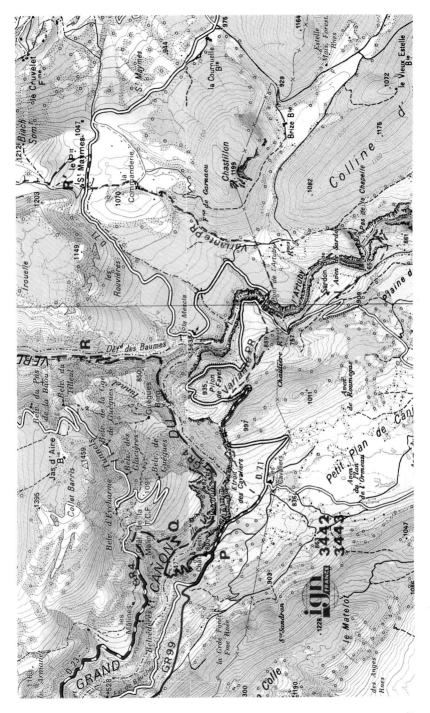

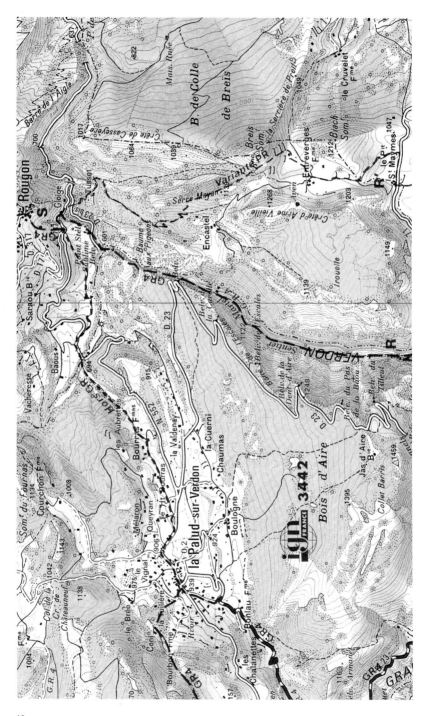

winding defiles: this encourages erosion which is as harmful to the soil and vegetation as it is dangerous to walkers.

The GR99 ends here. To find accommodation and provisions, walkers need to follow the GR4 either west or east.

A description of the GR4 (westwards) begins on p. 49.

The GR4 (eastwards) is described, though in reverse direction, in Walk 2.
In 10 hours 45 minutes you reach Castellane. After 5 hours 30 minutes you reach Chalet du Point Sublime, 787m — S on the map. It has a hotel with restaurant (closed in winter), a campsite and a taxi. 30 minutes further on you come to Rougon (930 metres), with campsite, provisions and water. Other accommodation is possible — ask at the *mairie*.

Warning: walkers on the GR coming from the opposite direction must stock up on water and food here, as they are not available in the Gorges du Verdon.

A further 4 hours 45 minutes takes you to Castellane, 724m.

CASTELLANE

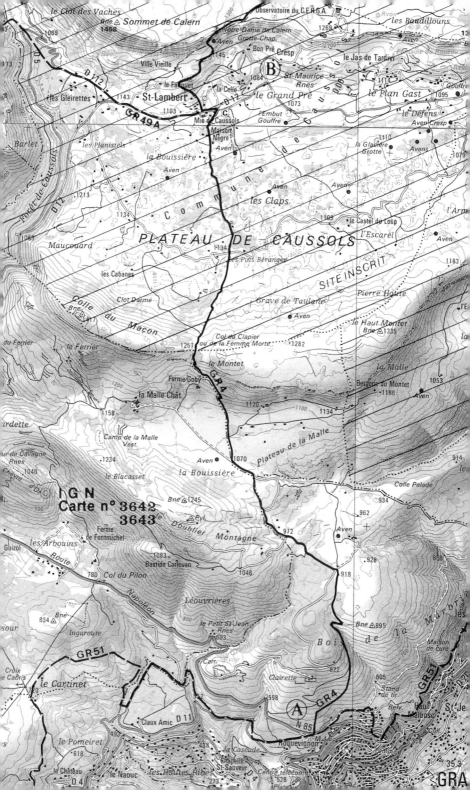

WALK 2

GRASSE

🏠 ⌂ ⚠ ✕ 🍷
🚊 🚋 ℹ

333m

*Grasse is a sous-préfecture
of the Alpes-Maritimes.
World capital of the perfume
industry, the town is
surrounded by fields of
flowers. The old town, a real
labyrinth of little streets and
steps, has hardly changed
since the 18th century. :
Cathedral; town hall (l'Hôtel
de Ville); Fragonard
museum.*

1:45

Plateau de la Malle
910m

0:45

Col du Clapier
1260m

1:30

CAUSSOLS
(Saint-Lambert)
🏠 ✕ 🚊
1150m

2:15

At the beginning of the GR4 you will find the red and white marking of the GR51, 'Balcons de la Côte d'Azur', which leads to Théoule and the Esterel massif in the west, and to the east, the GR5 to Aspremont (near Nice) and the GR52 to Castellar (near Menton) and Italy. The GR4 starts north of the town (map ref A), above the swimming stadium and near the tennis courts; you can take a local bus to this point. Take a footpath northwards, then follow a tarmacked road westwards for 200 metres, and a path northwards which joins the Chemin de la Malle. Walk along this as far as the Plateau de la Malle.

The GR4 follows a little-used road with a short-cut across it. About 300 metres further on (1070m), having passed the road to the Château de la Malle, continue northwards on a footpath which crosses the Ferriers ridge to the Col du Clapier.

Take a footpath going down to the Plateau de Caussols, a barren, fissured limestone plateau, which you cross by road as far as Caussols (Saint-Lambert).

In front of the *mairie*, cross the D12 and go up to the left to the Plan du Fanguet; there, turn right in order to reach a small peak (at 1272 metres). You will see the CERGA observatory to the east. Pass between a ruin and a well (which is often dry), and proceed towards a large cairn, which marks the border between the districts of Caussols and Cipières. Arriving at the cairn, turn right (east) and remaining at almost the same level, walk along by the CERGA installation. Cross a track and take the footpath to the left (north-east), which goes down along the small valley of a dried-up river. A bit further down, the GR changes banks and continues to lose height, reaching another track. Take the track to the right and, using the footpath, descend the coomb. You will pass a natural arch and will see below a spring in the rocks, and wells. The footpath continues

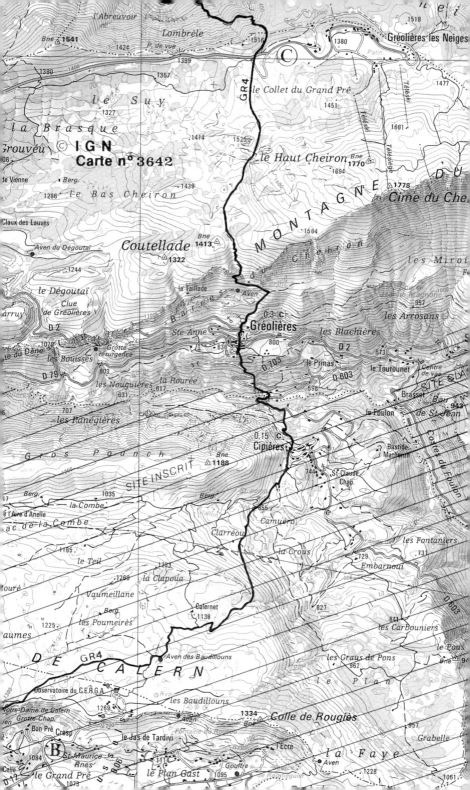

towards the north-east, crosses a hilltop and descends rapidly to the valley of Les Presses. Continue along the opposite bank and along a little dirt track to Cipières.

CIPIÈRES

🏠 ⛲

780m
Picturesque little village overlooking the right bank of the River Loup.

There is a good road going down to the Loup, which you cross on an old bridge. Continue for 400 metres along a minor road, then go left on a footpath which will cut across the D703 road twice. After crossing the road the second time, the footpath takes off again beside an iron gate, where a path emerges. The making of this path has destroyed the footpath in some places, but the way is well marked out. This takes you to Gréolières.

GRÉOLIÈRES

Ⓗ ⛲ 🚌

820m
Picturesque Provençal village situated at the foot of the Cime du Cheiron (1778 metres).
Church contains interesting late 14th century reredos of Saint-Étienne (School of Nice).

Climb up to Haut-Gréolières, then, by a path which crosses the Barres du Cheiron (ridges), you arrive at the Pas de Coutellade (1500 metres). From there, go down to the Baisse du Grand-Pré (1360 metres), thence to the road which serves Gréolières-les-Neiges (map ref C).

Route de Gréolières-les-Neiges

Warning: the section of the route from the Baisse du Grand-Pré to Vegay may be tricky if it is snowing.

Cross the road and climb up to a peak (1400 metres). Using a steep, narrow footpath across

---

The Villages

These are the villages of light, made up of bright houses, their lines reduced to essentials, with stone-coloured mortar: there are no shrill tones, no false notes. They are all protected from the whims of fashion which, intending to 'adorn', merely disfigure. They are nearly all assembled on cliffs, like Le Vieux-Mont-Salier or Sault, or on rocky peaks like Aurel, Banon, Simiane: those were fortified in the Middle Ages and have kept at least some of their châteaux, towers and ramparts. Inside the villages, especially at Simiane, you will find the town-houses of the 16th, 17th or 18th centuries, with their handsome doorways, their stone staircases, their vast and sober rooms . . .

Other villages are spread out in the sun, peacefully dispersed amidst fields and hills: le Revest, le Contadour, les Hautes-Ferrassières, le Plan de Montsalier . . . Or like the admirable hamlets of Dauban and Chavon, whose functional tangle of buildings is a work of art, the result of centuries of labour.

Detour *45 mins*
STATION DE
1:15 GRÉOLIÈRES-LES-NEIGES
🏠
Summit of Le Cheiron (1778 metres); easy access, chairlift.

the woods, descend westwards as far as a little gully, where the path improves and follows a coomb. In the distance you will see the Compagnie des Eaux (water company) building; walk up to it, and continue to the deserted houses of Vegay.

Vegay
930m
Detour *45 mins*
Aiglun
642 metres.
1:30 *After the bridge, turn right, cross the Esteron and go up by a winding path as far as the D10.*

Then follow a path as far as the waterfall of Vegay, and go down to the River Gironde, which you cross near its confluence with the River Esteron (457 metres).

Climb up the other bank by a footpath going west, which reaches the D10; take the D10 to the left (west). Leave the road after a hairpin bend for a footpath to the right (north) which climbs to the hamlet of La Clue.

La Clue
1

The footpath goes across a mass of rocks and then a rocky spur, woods and undergrowth to reach the Crête de Charamel.

Crête de Charamel
1155m

A winding footpath leads down from the Crête de Charamel. Ignore a footpath on the left and continue down to the ruined hamlet of Abdoun (Adom on the map). Here the path heads west and descends (north) to the Esteron, which it crosses. Continue straight on towards a copse, and walk alongside it for 200 metres.

1:45

The markings for the GR4 continue along the Fontaine stream, which you ford to climb up to the D2211a. Take this road left as far as Collongues.

COLLONGUES
⌂ ✕ ⚖

628m

Junction with the GR des Huit Vallées (Eight Valleys). Same route as the GR4 to Amirat.

Follow the D2211a in the direction of Briançonnet; about 1 kilometre from Collongues, go right (north-west) along a path which crosses a private estate (keep to the marked path). Cross the Cressonière stream, then pass beneath an electric cable at the level of Le Colombier sheepfold. The path swings east and reaches Amirat.

AMIRAT
⌂

850m

Leave the village by the D83 going west, then continue on a footpath situated below this road as far as a transformer. Here, you cross the D83 to get to a road, surfaced for 100 metres, which climbs to a *collet* then crosses the Ravin du Passé (not marked on map). The GR4 continues along a path, leaving the footpath to the Col du Buis on the left and a bit later, that of the Col de Trébuchet (both not marked). Climb up to the Crête de Chadastier.

Crête de Chadastier
1150m

Attention: hikers accompanied by dogs are reminded to keep them on a leash when crossing pastures with sheep. The passage of the GR has been authorised by the shepherds.

The GR goes down the north slope of the Crête de Chadastier: first to the right and then to the left (west). You will meet up with a canal, which you follow as far as the hamlet of l'Hubac (l'Ubac) d'Amirat (map ref E), where water is obtainable. Go through the hamlet and when you reach the end, head right and then in a north-easterly direction, going down a little path across the meadows as far as the edge of the forest, to meet a footpath leading to the Ravin du Pestre.

Ravin du Pestre
820m

From the bridge, the GR takes a farm path lined with chestnut trees which goes between the château-farm and a washing-place to reach the D10 in the hamlet of Castellat-Saint-Cassien.

Castellat-Saint-Cassien

Alternative route from Castellat-Saint-Cassien to Entrevaux. Setting out from the telephone box in Castellat, take the D10 eastwards in the direction of the Col du Trébuchet. You will

1:15

1

1

3

La Bastide Neuve

0:45

pass an oratory and then cross a Roman bridge; 10 metres after that, take the forest track on the left (surfaced for 50 metres) rising to a pass (1100 metres). At the end of the field there is a ruined farm.

Walk behind this ruin and follow a path on the mountainside which heads north-east; after a kilometre, this path turns sharp left to the other slope of the mountain. A diagonal descent takes you to a road in front of the Moréno estate, which you take to the left as far as the D911. Take this down to Entrevaux.

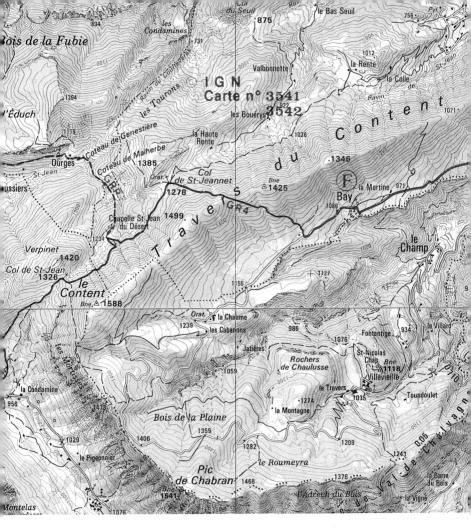

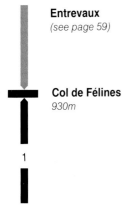

Entrevaux
(see page 59)

Col de Félines
930m

1

From Castellat-Saint-Cassien, the GR4 takes the D10 westwards; after a kilometre, it arrives at another road; here, climb up to the right on a forest path which meets the road at the Col de Félines.

Cut across the D911 to follow the grassy footpath opposite, which soon turns right. After about 1.5 kilometres, you reach a bend in the road (just after 812 on map). Take the road for 200 metres, then turn left on a path which cuts cross two bends and goes down a rocky gully, which you cross. You thus reach a rocky ledge which comes out at a bend in the road. Take to the road again; 150 metres further on, leave it

for a little path on the left, which cuts across the bends. You will come back to the road at the entrance to the little town of Entrevaux.

ENTREVAUX

ⓗ ⌂ ⛺ ✕ 🚉 ☎ 🚌

480m

A little town of 700 inhabitants situated on the left bank of the River Var. Until 1860, it occupied a strategic position as the frontier town between French Provence and the States of the King of Sardinia. It had been fortified by Vauban who, between 1692 and 1706, remodelled the Citadel.
Old town, which is especially picturesque; ancient cathedral.

3

The GR de Pays GTPA (Grande Traversée des Préalpes), passes this way. It shares the course of the GR4 as far as the chapel of Saint-Jean-du-Désert. Coming out of the town, take the D610 to Le Champ and Villevielle. At the first bend, leave it for a footpath to the right which cuts across the bends, then continues along a path lined by low stone walls, keeping south-west, parallel to the little road leading to the hamlet of Bay (map ref F). You will arrive at the chapel of Saint-Claude (Bay); follow the road for about 1 kilometre, then turn right (north-west) on to a footpath which climbs through an oakwood. You will come out on a sort of plateau. From here you can see a fine beech grove, through which you go down to the Col de Saint-Jeannet.

Col de Saint-Jeannet
1278m

The footpath descends to a forest, passes an overflowing spring, crosses a meadow and reaches the chapel of Saint-Jean-du-Désert (1251 metres).

0:45

This priory is maintained by the monks of the Lérins Abbey, who make pilgrimages here on 24 June and 29 August.

This is the junction with the GR de Pays GTPA (marked in yellow and red), which heads north towards Sisteron. The GR4 proceeds south-west and continues through the forest as far as the Oratoire Saint-Jean (not labelled).

Oratoire Saint-Jean
1321m

1:15

From the oratory cut to the right across the undergrowth towards the road below and the chapel of Notre-Dame de la Rivière (958 metres). Cross a wooden bridge to reach the D10, which you take to the right for 400 metres as far as another bridge. Immediately after this bridge, go left along a stony road leading to the village of Ubraye.

UBRAYE
⌂
1000m

From the square, go left along a road which skirts the church; a little street cuts across the bends to descend to the lower part of the village, situated in a little pass. Take the path between the houses which rises to the right across the *garrigue* planted with pines. You will thus reach the new Le Touyet road near a bend, the construction of which has destroyed

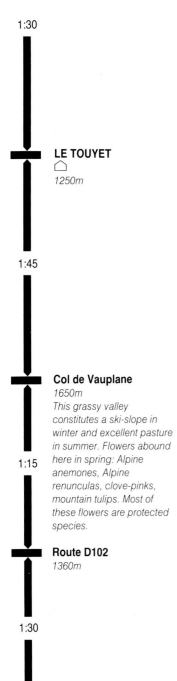

1:30

LE TOUYET
⌂
1250m

1:45

Col de Vauplane
1650m
This grassy valley
constitutes a ski-slope in
winter and excellent pasture
in summer. Flowers abound
here in spring: Alpine
anemones, Alpine
renunculas, clove-pinks,
mountain tulips. Most of
these flowers are protected
species.

1:15

Route D102
1360m

1:30

the original path. Go up along the road for several dozen metres as far as this bend, to the left of which a small linking path has been marked out to join up with the old pathway. Go up the mountainside overlooking the valley of La Bernade. You go past a hilltop. You can see the village of Le Touyet from a path on the hillside, below the road; this takes you to the village of Le Touyet.

At the first house, take the footpath on the right which passes before the oratory, then follow the road as far as the last house in the hamlet. Then take the path going up to the right, then, to the left, walk along by the ruined house. You will pass an oratory (1282 metres). The easy, pleasant path winds gently upwards amidst the lavender; you can see the verdant plateau of La Palud to the left. The GR separates off from the footpath 1 kilometre after the oratory; it goes left, crosses a *roubine* and goes down to the stream, La Bernade, which it crosses (1416) metres). The path twists upwards through a mass of rocks) the well marked path climbs the slope, passes near a cabin and reaches the large, grassy shelf of the Col de Vauplane.

Follow the road for 300 metres and, when it leaves the plain, take the footpath to the right which goes up the slope. Go left and downwards to the river; follow it as far as the chapel of Saint-Barnabé (1381 metres). Cross a canal, go along by the fields and pass by the sheepfolds to reach the D102.

Go along a very broad footpath opposite, which runs alongside an electricity line on the edge of a forest. There is a panoramic view over the village of Demandolx and the two artificial lakes of Castillon and Chaudanne. The footpath passes the foot of a pylon, then a deep hollow at the foot of Le Teillon. It becomes narrower as it crosses a stream, which is often dry. Five minutes from the stream, you have a view of a bridge whose architecture is unique in Europe. The footpath continues as far as Clot d'Agnon.

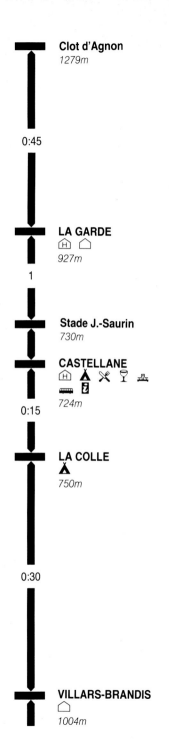

Clot d'Agnon
1279m

0:45

LA GARDE
ⓗ ⌂
927m

1

Stade J.-Saurin
730m

CASTELLANE
ⓗ ⛺ ✗ 🍷 ⛴
🚌 🅱
724m

0:15

LA COLLE
⛺
750m

0:30

VILLARS-BRANDIS
⌂
1004m

When you reach a big pylon, there are two possible ways of getting to Castellane: 1) the former GR4 route, kept as an alternative, passing the chapel of Saint-Roch and the cité de Chaudanne (dotted line); 2) the new GR4 route, described below.

New GR4 route from Clot d'Agnon to Castellane. At the pylon, abandon the forest path going straight down to the bottom of the valley in favour of the path which, crossing the north-facing side of the Clot d'Agnon, then the Adret des Gravières, descends to La Garde.

Take the N85 west in the direction of Castellane for about 500 metres. Then go down to the left by a path which, downhill from the road, comes out on a minor road; follow that as far as the N85, which you will rejoin near the J.-Saurin stadium.

The GR4 runs alongside the N85; cross the bridge over the Verdon to enter Castellane.

At Castellane, the GR4 goes along the road behind the Hôtel du Verdon. Cross the Listes plain on a surfaced road, turning right to meet the D952 or 'Route des gorges', and go to the left along that; 200 metres further on, take the road on the right up to the hamlet of La Colle.

Take the bridge across the stream and continue along the access road to the hamlet of Villars-Brandis, which overlooks the route des gorges and even further down, the River Verdon. Where a footpath goes off to the right, near a little quarry (at the 857 metre point), hikers are offered two choices: 1) the former GR4 route, kept as an alternative, which follows the Roman way on the mountainside (dotted line on the map); 2) the new route via Villars-Brandis, described below.

New route to Col de la Chapelle Saint-Jean via Villars-Brandis. Go up to the right on a little road through the undergrowth which meets a twisting road. Follow it to the right as far as Villars-Brandis.

Upstream from the village, go to the left on a winding footpath which leads to the hamlet of Brandis, now in ruins, at the foot of the rocky

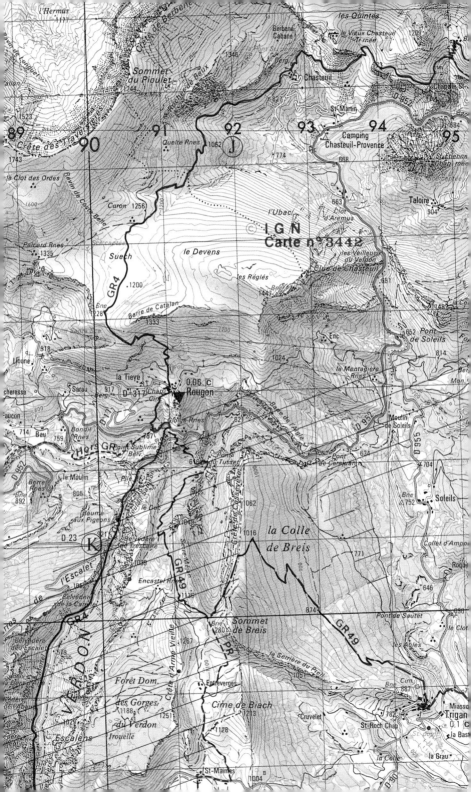

cliffs known as 'Cadières de Brandis'. Near a number of 'tables à sel' (salt flats), you will find a twisting footpath on the left which goes down to meet the alternative route at the edge of the Brandis gully.

The GR continues along the mountainside on the Roman way and reaches the chapel of Saint-Jean pass.

Col de la Chapelle Saint-Jean
950m
Detour *10 mins*
Chapelle Saint-Jean

Keep following the Roman way along the mountainside, to arrive at Chasteuil.

0:45

Chasteuil
900m
A picturesque village, perched on the mountainside overlooking the valley of Verdon. Now inhabited by young artisans – potters, workers in stone, wood and leather.

1

Detour *20 mins*
ROUTE DES GORGES
▲ ✗ ♨

Pass the former school of Chasteuil, below the château of the Comte de Chasteuil. The Roman way goes into a beautiful oak forest, which gives way to a moor covered in broom; you will notice in passing some walls dating back to Roman times. Emerging from the wooded area, you pass a dried-up spring on the right, and 500 metres further on you reach a pass.

Col
1200m
This pass is situated between two rounded massifs, and offers a panoramic view: to the east the village of Talloire, nestling at the foot of the Pic de Talloire, La Montagne de Robion, and the famous Cadières de Brandis.

After the pass, the footpath runs alongside a grassy dip, where two sheepfolds offer possible shelter. To the north you will find the beginnings of two footpaths: one of them leads to the summit of the Moure de Chanier. Pass beneath two electricity lines and go down a broad path to the village of Rougon.

1

ROUGON
⌂ ▲ ♨
930m
Junction with the GR49 coming from Fréjus.

Pass beneath the village and, near a washing-place, take a short-cut which gets you to a crossroads and the Chalet du Point Sublime.

0:20

CHALET DU POINT SUBLIME
⌂ Å ✕

787m

Detour *10 mins*
Point Sublime belvedere
From this lookout you can admire the Couloir Samson and the River Verdon flowing through it, 100 metres below.

Detour, see left. From the Point Sublime the GR4 goes south, then west, then north in a horseshoe through the Gorges du Verdon. The passage through the Gorge is the most difficult and dangerous part of the walk (a larger-scale map, IGN blue series 3442 est, is recommended). The route is described later.

A far easier alternative is to cut across southwest to La Palud-sur-Verdon (not way-marked, but indicated on the map).

Detour *2 hours*
La Palud-sur-Verdon

Detour, see left. Go along the footpath leading to the Point Sublime belvedere for several metres, then turn right on to a path descending to the Baux stream, and walk alongside it as far as the D952. Take this to the left towards La Palud; 200 metres further on, before a bridge, take a path to the right and directly afterwards, having crossed a stream, take a footpath on the left running alongside a wooded area overlooking the Angles gully. You will pass Les Bourras farm, and other farms nearby, to come out on the D952, which you follow to the right as far as La Palud-sur-Verdon.

Alternative route through the Gorges of Verdon to La Palud-sur-Verdon.

Important: This route should only be undertaken in good weather. You should allow 7 hours for the whole trip between Point Sublime and La Mâline. Beware of falling stones near the cliffs, they can be dislodged in stormy weather, and avoid the metal ladders during thunderstorms. An electric torch is indispensible for going through the tunnels.

In the course of this route the hiker will encounter 7 tunnels, dug out 70 years ago when a dam was planned; fortunately it was never built, as this site would have been flooded. Only the first 2 tunnels, on the way from Point Sublime, are to be used; avoid the other tunnels which have partly caved in and are therefore dangerous.

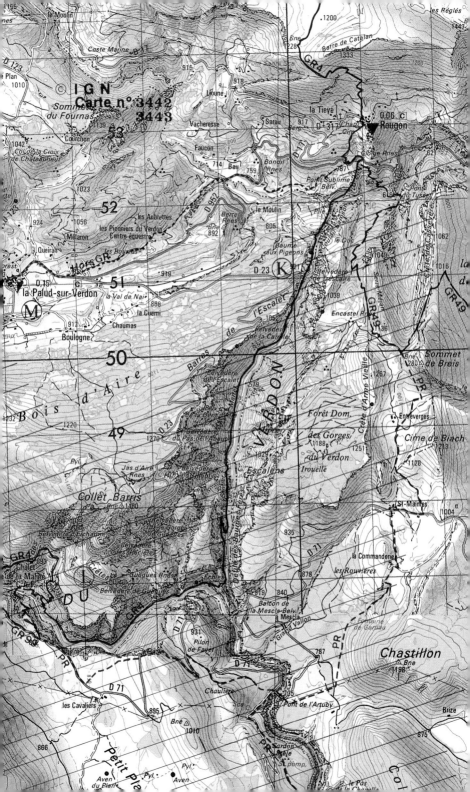

0:30

Entry to the
Gorges du Verdon
600m
*Departure point for the
'Sentier Martel'.*

0:45

Tunnel de Trescaïre
*This tunnel is 100 metres
long.*

1:30

Warning: Across the screes (Estellié, Guègues), follow the marked path with extreme care, because a direct descent will destroy the footpath and make the ascent difficult for walkers coming from the opposite direction.

From the Chalet du Point Sublime, the GR4 follows the D952 towards Castellane; 200 metres further on, it leaves the road for a footpath going down to the right as far as the D23bis; take this road to the right to reach the parking area at the entrance to the Gorges du Verdon.

From the entry to the Gorges du Verdon, the GR4 goes down across rocks and scree to reach a stream (a branch of the River Verdon), which it crosses on a footbridge. A little further on, go up the steps to the entry to the first tunnel, called 'Le Baou', and go into it. This tunnel, 670 metres long, is in the form of an S. You pass two windows allowing a view of the 'Couloir Samson'. At about 400 metres from the tunnel entrance, near a third window, you can take the stairs down to the 'Baume aux Pigeons' (Pigeons' Cave, map ref K).

Warning: on the left (if you are coming from Point Sublime) you will find a steeply sloping chute which served as the rubble-deposit when the tunnel was being dug; take great care not to slide into that.

After you have made your way through the first tunnel, shortly after the exit (when coming back, beware of the narrowing walls which form the Couloir Samson), you go into the second tunnel, the Tunnel de Trescaïre.

At the exit to this tunnel, continue along the horizontal path; cross the scree. Ignore the third tunnel, called the 'Baume'; on the other side of the Verdon you can see two dolomitic towers which mark the end of the 'Chaos de Trecaïre'. The gorge widens; the footpath goes up and down, following the 'Rue d'eau du Verdon' (the water road).

Warning: do not go through the next 3 tunnels; there is danger of their caving in.

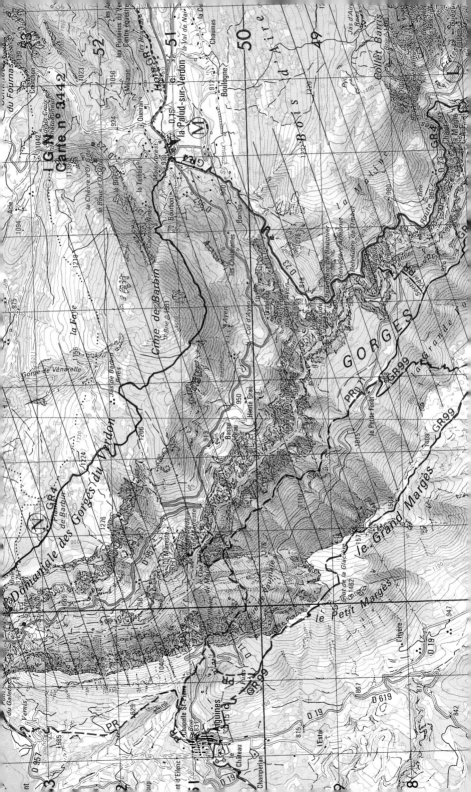

Avoid the fourth tunnel, called the 'Escalès', and the fifth, called the 'Clapier' and finally the sixth, the 'Bari' (see left). You now arrive at the entrance to the seventh tunnel, called the 'Guèges' or the 'Artuby'.

Tunnel des Guèges, or de l'Artuby

The tunnel is situated 50 metres above the footpath. If the weather is bad, or night is approaching, you can take this tunnel and thus avoid the Brèche Imbert (gap) and its ladders.

0:10

The GR4 leaves this tunnel and takes a path going down to a footpath, whose gentle descent it follows to the right. You arrive above a sandy beach.

Plage de Sable
(Sandy beach)

After going along a footpath running slightly above the Verdon, climb up to the right on a winding footpath. You pass in turn the 'Baume aux Chiens' and the 'Baume aux Hirondelles' (caves of the dogs and of the swallows, hollowed out of the cliff). Then you reach the foot of the metal ladders (6 in number), which you climb in order to reach the Brèche Imbert (Imbert gap).

Brèche Imbert

This gap allows the crossing of the rocky spur of the Mescla. It gives a splendid view over the course of the Verdon. Go left (south) as far as the place from which you can see the Mescla to the right and, to the left, the Défilé des Baumes Frères and the Rue d'eau du Verdon as far as the Chaos de Trescaïre (not on the map).

0:30

Go down the footpath as far as the crossroads of the Mescla footpath.

Warning: several of the next places are not marked on the map, so care should be taken.

Sentier de la Mescla
Detour *15 mins,*
The site of the Mescla.

Take the footpath to the left (south-east), several metres above the Verdon. You will reach the site of the Mescla, which means the meeting of the waters, where there is a confluence of the Verdon and the Artuby. This is one of the most characteristic sites of the Canyon of the Verdon.

0:40

The GR4 continues to the foot of the rocky wall. Coming back, you will see the high wall of the Mescla, and reach the Baume aux Boeufs (not on the map).

Baume aux Boeufs

A vast cave, where you can camp, and from which you can descend to the Verdon

0:15

Éboulis des Guègues

(not marked on the map).

0:40

Pré de l'Issane

A green oasis where the vegetable outweighs the mineral, a relatively rare state in the Verdon Canyon.

0:40

Carrefour de l'Estellié

You can see the Estellié footbridge opposite, which enables you to cross the Verdon. You will find here the markings for the GR99. (Dotted line on map.)

1

CHALET DE LA MÂLINE

△

2   *900m*

LA PALUD-SUR-VERDON

🏠 △ ⚐ ✕ ♨

🚐 🅿

950m

1:30

Source de Barbin

1330m

0:30

Jas de Barbin

1210m

The GR4 climbs in three loops to the Éboulis des Guègues.

This is situated at the exit of the seventh tunnel, called the 'Guègues' or the 'Artuby', which hikers can go through to avoid the Brèche Imbert (not marked) and its ladders. The footpath descends gently to the Étroit des Cavaliers, after which it comes out at the Pré de l'Issane (meadow).

The GR4 continues along a footpath running about 30 metres above the Verdon. Across a wood, it reaches the Carrefour de l'Estellié.

The GR4 turns right and climbs through an oakwood to the foot of a metal ladder. Climb the ladder to cross the rocky ridge of the Pas de l'Issane. The footpath climbs northwards to cross the gully of Le Charençon and then turns west. Pass below the parking area and then you reach the Chalet de la Mâline.

The GR4 takes the D23 as far as La Palud-sur-Verdon.

Take the Châteauneuf-les-Moustiers road; at an oratory, go left up a road which climbs to a wooded area. You will pass the back of a farm; go down to the left then climb up a gully in the direction of the forest. You pass between a sheepfold and an almond-tree, then wind your way up the Barbin mountain. Pass the dried-up Bouens spring; the footpath goes up the southern face of Barbin and overlooks the Col d'Ayen on the Gorges road. You reach a small pass and the Barbin spring.

A bit further on, take the forest track going down through the pines. You will join the forest path, and in a clearing find the Jas be Barbin.

First of all go left then, 300 metres further on, go right. Further on, cross the track coming from the Gorges de Venarelle. You find it again a bit further down, where you follow it to the right. After having gone through a second

1

0:30

Col de Plein Voir
1200m
View of the lake of Sainte-
Croix, the Lure mountain,
and in the distance, the
Luberon, the massif of
Sainte-Victoire and Mont
Ventoux.

Col de l'Ane
1095m

1:30

Route des Gorges
570m

1:15

MOUSTIERS-SAINTE-MARIE
⌂ ⌂ ⚑ ✕ ⚏
🅱
631m
A town renowned for its
pottery, built on a site of
outstanding beauty.

1:15

small valley, you reach the Plaine de Barbin (map ref N). Continue as far as the crossroads of the tracks, then turn right. A little further on, take a forest track leaving from a pinewood on the right. You will then pass the ruined cabins of Le Mout (not labelled). A little later, you reach the Plein Voir (Good View) pass.

Ignore the path to the right and the left and continue along the crest, passing 2 high-tension cables, as far as the Col de l'Ane (Donkey Pass).

After the Col de l'Ane, the GR4 keeps going along the crest. You pass the Signal de l'Ourbes (1216 metres), then descend to the rocky ridges above the Ferme de Beylière. You then reach the Gorges road (D952).

Several short-cuts will get you to the crossing of the roads from Aiguines, Castellane and Moustiers-Sainte-Marie where there is a camp-site (see map). Follow the Moustiers-Sainte-Marie road to the Chapelle Saint-Pierre. After another 200 metres take a south-west path to the left; 200 metres further on, turn right and 500 metres further again, you will come out on a path which the GR4 takes to the left (south-west) towards the plateau. If you turn right (north), you reach the village of Moustiers-Sainte-Marie. If you carry straight on, you will reach the *gîte*.

The markings begin again at the centre of the town at the Hôtel Belvédère. Follow the N592 (the Castellane road) for 50 metres, then fork to the right on a minor road (dotted line on map); ignore the right-hand road to the Château Saint-Jean. Keep going south, and you will soon reach the hollow of the valley. Leaving the ferme du Colombier on the left, ford the Maïre stream. Cross the gully of Les Graves (537 metres) by a dirt track, and climb up the opposite side by a winding forest path. You will thus arrive at the plateau.

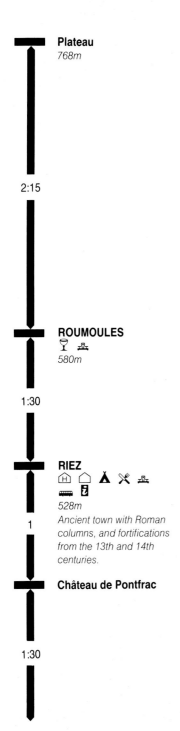

Plateau
768m

2:15

ROUMOULES
580m

1:30

RIEZ
528m
Ancient town with Roman columns, and fortifications from the 13th and 14th centuries.

Château de Pontfrac

1:30

Turn left for 50 metres following the Moustiers-Sainte-Marie road to Sainte-Croix-de-Verdon. Then take a minor road to the left, which soon becomes a dirt track. For about 2 kilometres the path runs alongside the edge of a forest which covers the slopes down as far as the lake of Sainte-Croix. When the path leaves the edge of the forest, the GR turns right (west). The GR reaches a surfaced road 400 metres on, which it takes to the right for about 100 metres to Chandon. It then turns left, passing beneath two electricity lines. The GR4 continues on the road which goes across the Plaine des Bessons, with its vast fields of cereals and lavender. Passing the Roubion farm on your left, you will reach a crossroads (677 on the map); turn left on the path here and, 500 metres further on, to the right (west) onto a tarmacked path which goes along the ridge between two gullies and descends to Roumoules.

Go right through the village, cut across the N592, take the Puimoisson road, cross the Calostre and 250 metres further on, turn left on to a dirt track rising to the plateau. At the first crossroads, take the path to the left which crosses the Plaine de Sainte-Maxime amidst fields of lavender. You will reach the chapel of Sainte-Maxime, situated on a hill overlooking the valley of the Colostre. Go down to Riez.

Leave Riez by the Valensole road (D6), which you follow for 3 kilometres. When the road sweeps round to the right, to climb to the Valensole plateau, take a road which goes straight on; 400 metres further on, it reaches the Château de Pontfrac.

Continue along the dirt track. After about 1500 metres, leave this for a stony path rising quite steeply towards the plateau. Walk through the woods alongside the footpath to the left. When you reach the level of Le Jas du Truy, walk between the cultivated fields to reach Le Jas, then continue along a dirt track. At the crossroads, go left on the path which runs through various fields for about 2 kilometres. After this the path changes direction several times, and descends directly south as far as the D15.

D15

1:30

SAINT-MARTIN-DE-BRÔMES

370m
Romanesque church; 13th century Templars' tower; Gallo-Roman museum.

2

Follow the D15 to the right; 50 metres further on (580), take the fire-break dirt track to the left. This follows the Crête (ridge) de Saint-Pierre, first of all across cultivated land, then across a wooded section. Pass under an electricity line and, 800 metres further on, take the path to the right which, a little further on, crosses in a straight line land planted with young olive-trees. You then go through the undergrowth before going down again to the village of Saint-Martin-de-Brômes.

Leave the village westwards by the D952, which goes over a little bridge; 100 metres further on, when it veers to the left, continue straight ahead on a tarmacked path which rises rapidly towards the plateau. Take the right-hand fork and a bit further on, go left. The footpath crosses fields of lavender then a forest. Arriving at a crossroads, take the broad forest path on the right, which goes down in the direction of Gréoux-les-Bains and the Verdon. At a crossroads, the GR turns left (directly south) leaving the mas Ferrier on the right. Cut across the D952, and continue opposite on a road which meets up with the Verdon. Turn right; the GR runs alongside the Verdon on a dirt track to the area of the hydropathic establishment of Gréoux-les-Bains.

GRÉOUX-LES-BAINS

400m; this is the 'thermal capital' of Haute-Provence, with its sulphurous waters. Templars' château, whose heavy mass is visible from all directions. Its site was a fortified Roman post, and historians agree that it was built by the Templars.

2

Towards the year 1120 the Order came to the alps of Haute-Provence and was installed at Gréoux. The estates passed through various families until the French Revolution, when the lands and the Château de la Seigneurie de Gréoux were sold as national property.

Les Quatre Chemins
294m

1:30

MANOSQUE

350m
The town is situated at the foot of hills covered in olive trees and overlooking the alluvial plain of the Durance. Manosque was a Ligurian oppidum on Hercules' road. It is suggested that the name originates in manec *(full of springs) and* asq *(river). Church of Saint-Saveur, where you will find the Black Virgin of Manosque, the*

0:30

Go through the town to reach the picturesque little streets spread out on the hill overlooked by the château. Behind this, take a stony path which rises rapidly to the plateau; 2 kilometres further on, you will meet the D82, which you follow to the right; 800 metres further on, take a sheltered footpath to the left which provides glimpses over the valley of the Durance. You arrive in sight of the Mas Devenson; go down a hillock planted with thyme and take a wide dirt track, leaving a *mas* below on the right. Descend rapidly on the right-hand road; 50 metres further on, turn left on to a path going up to the *mas* du Grand Devenson (not labelled on map). After the *mas* du Grand Devenson, you cross arable land and go down to the Manosque road (D6), which you take to the left; 700 metres further on, you reach the vicinity of Les Quatres Chemins (Four Paths).

The GR4 takes the D907 and crosses the River Durance on the 'Pont de Manosque'; 800 metres further on, turn right and go through the installation for crushing shingle from the Durance (IGN ref 294). Carry straight on at the next crossroads (IGN ref 305). When you reach a copse, take the Chemin des Naïsses to the left, going over an irrigation canal (IGN ref 312). A bit further on, take the Avenue du Moulin Neuf, go under the railway line (the marking ends at this point) and continue along the avenue to enter Manosque.

Hikers will find the markings for the GR4 at the Pont des Hubacs; the GR cuts across the D907 and climbs up via the Montée de Toutes Aures, then by the road to the chapel of Saint-Pancrasse.

oldest in France. In times of drought people come to pray to her for rain.

Chapelle Saint-Pancrasse

445m

Otherwise known as Chapelle de Toutes Aures, because it is exposed to all the winds. Saint Pancrasse is the patron saint of Manosque and the chapel is a place of pilgrimage and the Easter festival of 'La Saucissonade' is held there. Good views over the Luberon, Manosque, the Durance valley and Ubaye in the distance on a clear day.

1:15

The route continues in a south-westerly direction along a track which narrows to a path descending a ridge through kermes oak trees and broom to reach a crossroads at height marker 360. Take the road on your right. After 50 metres, take the Montée de la Calade, for residents only, which climbs westwards to the village of Pierrevert.

PIERREVERT

420m

Old fortified town. Chapel Sainte-Patrie and 13th century church doors. Craft centre. Famous for its wines.

Go through the village of Pierrevert and at the Place Saint-jean, take a path down to the old windmill. When you reach a crossroads, take the tarmac path on your right (west). This path, known as the Chemin de la Bucelle, takes you down to a road, the D6 on to which you turn left. After 500 metres, cross a stream and take

2:15

MONTFURON

🚌

670m

1:45

Montjustin

550m

1:10

Chapel of Notre-Dame-de-Pitié de Céreste

Detour *5 mins*

CÉRESTE

🏠 ⌂ ♨ ✕ 🚌

At the side of the chapel, take the path heading westwards into the village of Cèreste. Very ancient town, inhabited by the Ligurians and the Romans. On the main route between Italy and

1:15

the second path on your right (north north-west) towards the Domaine de la Blaque. The path climbs up through the vineyards and pinewoods and higher up goes through oak thickets. The path becomes a tarmac track. Go past the chapel of Saint-Elzéar and the cemetery and you will come to the village of Montfuron.

Leave the village at the northern end and go past a recently restored windmill on your right. When you reach a crossroads, take the dirt track in the middle, which takes you to the junction of the D907 and the D956. Turn west on to the D956 towards La Bastide-des-Jourdans. When the road veers south, continue on the dirt track opposite. In the distance, you can make out the Luberon massif. The path continues across the hillsides and runs alongside the nature sanctuary of Marembrème where the flora and fauna are protected species. This brings you to the village of Montjustin.

The GR4 merges with the GR97 as far as Oppedette. The path does not go into the village of Montjustin but continues westwards along a dirt track towards La Roque Bastide. At the entrance to a *lavendin* field, leave the ridge and descend to a road opposite the Tulargue farm (not on the IGN at 1:50,000). At the end of this stretch, the path is lined with centuries old oak trees. Turn left on to the road and cross the little bridge over the Aiguebelle. The path climbs up to a transformer where you turn right immediately on to a dirt track which joins the N100 road at the chapel of Notre-Dame-de-Pitié de Céreste.

Leaving the chapel on your left, the route continues over the N100, going northwards. Shortly after crossing the road, you come to a little river, the Encrèime. Cross over the Roman bridge then go under the old railway bridge of the disused Cavaillon-Volx line. Then take the little road heading north-east for about 2.5 kilometres. Go past a building called Bel Air and cross a stream. Continue along the road heading north then veering eastwards to reach the Chapel of Grand Carluc.

Spain, it was a town of major importance. Ruined castle, walled old city.

Chapel of Grand Carluc

From this very ancient ruined priory, take the surfaced track which goes over a little bridge and a few metres further turns left (north) on to a path alongside a wood. After 500 metres, ignore a path off to the right and carry on until you come to a road. Turn right on to the road which passes the west end of the ancient country house of La Pourraque and to the east of the Reynier hill. Cross the bridge over the Grand Vallat. Climb northwards to reach a tarmac road and follow this road northwards for about 30 metres. Then turn left on to a dirt track and after 1 kilometre you will see below, to your right, next to a hundred year-old cherry tree, a square dovecote which still has a few *boulins* — horizontal pieces of wood, sealed into a wall — inside. After climbing for about 1 kilometre, you reach a road which you cross to take a path up to the left to the village of Sainte-Croix-à-Lauze.

1:15

Sainte-Croix-à-Lauze
600m
Romanesque church, 18th century wrought iron gates at the entrance to the manor. Unusual roofs made from calcareous tiles, hence the name Lauze.

The walk does not go through the village. To visit it, take a steep path off to the right. At the entrance to the village, climb up to the left along a winding path alongside a ruined retaining wall. Shortly afterwards, turn right (north) on to a stony path bordered by a little stone wall with a row of vertical stones along the top. The path winds through lavender

fields, past a path off to the left and an oak tree, continuing northwards. Go under an electricity cable with a wooden post and skirt a *lavandin* field to come out on a plateau. Carry on towards the buildings of the Domaine du Grand Blanc along a new path running parallel to the old one. After a crossroads, descend along a dirt track, passing below and to the east of the hamlet of Grand-Blanc.

Views to the west over the Gorges of Oppedette and the mountains of the Vaucluse, to the south over the Grand Luberon, to the north-west over Banon and Simiane-la-Rotonde, on the horizon to the north the ridge of the Lure mountain.

When you reach Grand-Blanc, continue along the road, round two bends. Further, turn off the road which goes down to the hamlet of Fenouillet (where the GR6 passes) and follow a stony, furrowed path to an oratory dedicated to Saint Joseph in 1938. Descend straight down to a transformer beside a road. The GR4 and GR97 converge with the GR6 from Vachères and Sisteron. All three descend to the village of Oppedette via the road off to the left (west).

WALK 3

SISTERON

⌂ ⌂ ▲ ✕ ⟨glass⟩
⚒ 🚌 🚋 🔋

500 m

*Picturesque town, situated in
an imposing valley of the
Durance, the great gateway
separating the Dauphiné
from Provence.
Ancient Romanesque
cathedral of Notre-Dame;
towers and remains of 14th
century ramparts; citadel,
with 13th century keep and
covered way; massive 16th
century fortifications.*

8Km
2

Leave Sisteron by taking the Chemin du Molard westwards. This begins behind the police station, where the route-markers also start. The path makes its twisting way through the wood as far as an old shelter (748 metres), where there is a view over the valleys of the Durance, the Jabron and the Lure mountain. The GR descends towards the west, then changes direction to the right and swiftly afterwards to the left. From this point the route follows the east-west ridge almost all the way. The undergrowth closes in, which makes the path difficult to distinguish at times, but it follows the line of the crest (849 metres). Keep going along the crest (west) and you will come to pylon 52 with a high-tension wire. Strike out across the green valley of the Buech and the village of Ribiers. The GR follows the boundary between the Hautes-Alpes and the Alps of Haute-Provence (916 metres), then descends quite quickly on the north flank of the ridge (the markers are widely spaced here, for lack of posts). Setting out again towards the west, you will reach a sign marking the Col de la Mairie.

Col de la Mairie

800m

4.5Km
1:30

Turn sharp left towards the south; follow the rocky riverbed of a stream that is normally dried up, then a path which becomes a road, as far as the hamlet of La Fontaine, where there is a spring. This is the junction with the GR946, which has come from Serres. (The two GRs share the route from here to Sisteron.) Although a vehicle road descends to the Jabron valley, the GR6 makes its way south across the fields, passing the farm at Les Clots, then runs east of the Château de Pécoule and reaches the D946. It follows this road to the right for about 200 metres before turning left along the D53, called the 'Route de Lure', which leads to the hamlet of La Tour.

LA TOUR

⌂ ✕ ⟨glass⟩

*Do not leave La Tour without
a supply of water; springs
are few and far between, and
dry up in summer. The next*

The GR leaves the surfaced road at the hamlet of La Tour, and rises westwards, gently at first but then steeply by a furrowed footpath. The horizon widens and in good weather you can see the glaciers of Le Pelvoux to the north. The footpath keeps rising, sometimes reduced to a

2Km
0:30

permanent spring is at Notre-Dame-de-Lure.

mere track between clumps of boxwood, heading south. There is a view over the ridge of Les Bauds, behind which you can make out the summit of Lure. The GR rounds a corner and reaches the Pas des Portes.

Pas des Portes
1080m

Access to this gap between the mountains of Soumiou and Pélégrine is by the 'grande callade', a metalled path which overlooks a deep gorge with luxuriant vegetation. The path threads the pass, climbs a small grassy valley (not many markers here) and joins a forest track, which you follow west as far as the Jas de Madame.

4Km
1:30

JAS DE MADAME
🏠
1164m
There is a spring at the foot of the gully.

Follow the forest track, then cross a gully where there are fossils in the marl. Now you enter the forest on the north slope of the Lure mountain. Disregarding tracks and roads, the GR rises rapidly in a diagonal across the slope to the north-east, cutting the D53 three times and, by an ascent through the scree resulting from the construction of the road, rejoining it at the Pas de la Graille.

3Km
0:50

Pas de la Graille
1597m

On the south slope, the GR lèaves the surfaced road to follow west (right) the line of the crest. There is no vegetation at all and there is often a very strong wind. The view spreads out as far as the geodesic signal on the summit of Lure.

5Km
1:15

Summit of Lure
1826m
IGN maps are sometimes available from the hut on the summit.

Continue westwards along the crest for about 1 kilometre, then begin the descent of the southern slope of Lure, crossing the lifts of a ski-resort. The GR then heads east across poor grazing land to reach the foot of the Combe de Lure, which it follows as far as the chapel of Notre-Dame-de-Lure.

4Km
1

NOTRE-DAME-DE-LURE
🏠
1236m
only the church, which is being restored, survives from the abbey built towards the end of the 12th century.

Climb up towards the road by a metalled path. Near a ruined sheepfold, before you reach the road, take a forest track, crossing an area which is being replanted with trees after a fire.

8Km
2

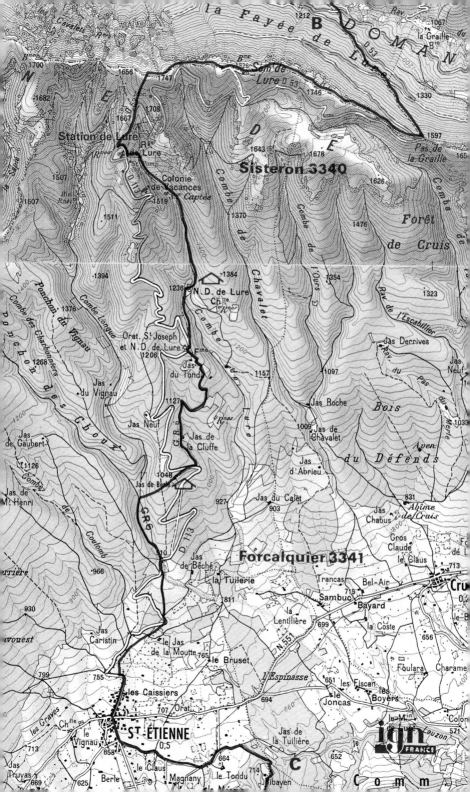

SAINT-ETIENNE-LES-ORGUES

🏠 ⛺ ✕ 🚉 🛈

6.5Km
2

700m
Old country chapel;
Romanesque church.

Fontienne

740m

1.5Km
0:20

LA PARISE

⌂

3Km
0:45

660m

FORCALQUIER

🏠 ⛺ ✕ 🍷 🚉
🚌 🛈

518m; ancient and
picturesque fortified town.
12th century church of
Notre-Dame; convent of
Cordeliers, part of the first
Franciscan foundation in
Provence; Porte des
Cordeliers, only remaining
section of ancient fortified
keep; ancient houses and a
fountain; museum; chapel of
Saint-Pancrace; cemetery
with yew-tree topiary.

MANE

🏠 ✕ 🚉 🚌

8Km
2

442m
Gallo-Roman relics;
16th century citadel;
11th century chapel of
Notre-Dame-de-Salagon is
being restored, and will
house the Conservatoire du
patrimoine ethnologique de
la Haute-Provence.

Leave the village by the D12. At the last houses, take the surfaced road on the left for 1.5 kilometres, then follow a forest path through a pinewood which comes out at the surfaced road from Revest. Take a dirt track to the right, which leads to the northern entry to Fontienne.

South of this hamlet, follow a cartroad ridge, which crosses a plateau covered in oaks; pass an isolated house, the Clot de Melly; continue by a good path across the wood as far as the area of Les Mourres, where there are curious rocks eroded into the shape of large heads. The GR6 leaves the path, turning left and taking a track which descends between the rocks and then makes for La Parise.

Descend straight to Forcalquier.

At the entrance to Forcalquier, take the little street on the left which leads to the exit from the town on the main road N100, which you follow right as far as the viaduct which spans the Viou ravine. Take the D950 towards Banon for about 700 metres, then turn left along a road which leads back to the N100 at the southern exit of Mane.

Follow the main road N100 for 100 metres, then turn right on to the road which leads to the Lac de la Laye. Go as far as the hamlet of La Laye, at the foot of the little valley. Cross the bridge and straight away turn left to take a dirt path along the valley. After you have forded the stream, take the path up to the Campagne de Châteauneuf. When you reach a barn (where it is strictly forbidden to camp), take the surfaced road to the right in the direction of the chapel which is 300 metres away. At the foot of the chapel, take the little path on the left and just before an oratory go

down a footpath on the left into the valley, and ford a stream. Climb up the other slope until you reach a path. Go right along the path, pass behind the Romanesque chapel of Saint-Jean and a little after that, turn left along a road which leads to the D305.

Detour

Follow the D305 to the right for 300 metres to reach the observatory of Haute-Provence, a large astronomical observatory belonging to the Centre National de la Recherche Scientifique (National Centre for Scientific Research). You can visit the observatory every Wednesday of the year, at 3 p.m. precisely.

The GR goes left down the D305 as far as the hamlet of Marceline, where it takes a path on the left parallel to the road, and rejoins the latter at the northern entrance to Saint-Michel-l'Observatoire.

SAINT-MICHEL-L'OBSERVATOIRE

🏠 ✕ 🍷 ⚓

536m

Romanesque church at top of village. Headquarters of the association 'Alpes de Lumière'.

8Km
2

Take a little street which begins in front of the church, and climb up the hill which overlooks the village; you will pass near the old church, then follow a path which leads to the D5; take this for several hundred metres, as far as the roads branching off to Aubenas-les-Alpes and Revest-des-Brousses. Go left on a footpath which descends among the oaks, then turn left along a little road which loops to join the bank of the Largue, which you cross near a pumping station. Continue westwards, climbing up a valley; after the Campagne farm, leave the surfaced road to take the path on your right, which winds up the hill; cross the D14 (735 metres) and by a little street enter Vachères.

VACHÈRES

⚓

820m

a medieval-looking village, with a 12th century church and Renaissance houses. On the small plateau which overlooks the village, there are the ruins of mills, a belvedere (861 metres) and traces of Gallo-Roman settlement.

6Km
1:30

Walk in front of the church and take a small road westward, with the plateau and its mills on your left. About 1.5 kilometres later, when the road heads left, continue along it but then turn right on a path which goes down to the farm at La Chaume; take the little surfaced road left. You will pass the hamlet of Tuilier and beneath the hamlet of Le Fenouillet. 600 metres further on is the junction with the GR4, which comes from Sainte-Croix-à-Lauze and enters Oppedette.

OPPEDETTE
🍷

500m; picturesque village, famous for the gorges which it overlooks. The base of the wayside calvary is an ancient votive altar to Mars, with interlaced pre-Roman carvings.

7Km
1:45

Detour
the Gorges d'Oppedette
The 'Alpes de Lumiere' association has made paths and route-marked the gorges. You can go round them in two circular walks, each of 2 hours duration; the upsteam circuit is marked in blue, the downstream circuit in yellow.

VIENS
⌂ 🍷 🚉 🚌
608m
medieval village in an eyrie, with handsome ramparts.

'Provençal Colorado'
The Colorado of Provence, so called because of the

10Km
2:30

similarities between its colours and those found in the famous region of the USA, is not a canyon, but a series of ocre quarries open to the sky. Erosion has shaped the coloured earth into strange forms. The site is criss-crossed with marked paths (described in Francois Morenas's guide Colorado provençal, *on sale locally).*

After the washing-place, the GR6 takes the little street which goes up on the left towards the plateau; follow the cliff line, go behind an old mill and cross a road to take the cartroad which runs parallel to it, and which the path ends up by joining. Take the D201 left for about 200 metres; turn right on a footpath which runs along the rim of the gorges as far as the bridge, then turn right along the little road which passes the Grosse-Blaque farm. This is the border of the Alpes-de-Haute-Provence with the Vaucluse. Continue along the road to the ruined chapel of Saint-Ferréol; after crossing a bridge, take a surfaced road left; it mounts the hill and leads to Viens.

Follow the D33 towards Banon for a kilometre, then turn left on a cart track which first runs parallel to the main road and then meets it at a bend; at that point take the path on your left lined with poplars, which descends the slope of a little wooded valley. After about 1 kilometre, you will be overlooking a deep hollow, with the hamlet of Gignac at the far end. This is the area called the 'Colorado' of Provence.

Warning: the marked paths of Colorado go through private property: do not deface the buildings, nor interfere with the dams nor walk across cultivated fields.

The GR descends to the right and follows the blue markings. When the tarmacked path makes a double bend, leave the blue line, which continues down to Gignac, and turn left. Soon you will overlook the white ridges of the Gignac quarries, which you skirt along the top; go right, past a house, to emerge on a main road coming from Gignac, which is marked in yellow dots. The GR6 and the yellow line follow the same route left along a path through pines and heather. In an enclosed, sandy valley, the two paths separate: the yellow line goes left and the GR6 descends to the right into another little valley which ends at a stream, the Doua, which you ford. Climb as far as a small road

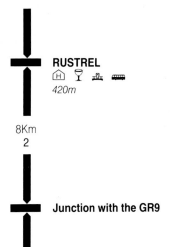

and go left along that; turn first right and, after cutting across the D22 you will reach the D30. Go left along it as far as Rustrel.

RUSTREL
420m

Go west along the street which leads out of the village; you will pass below the Château Duclos and join the D34, which you follow to the right for about 500 metres; then turn left on a road which crosses the D179, and walk through the hamlet of Les Viaux, where there is drinking water. Turn right, passing below the hamlet of Petits-Cléments; cross the road going up to Villars and go on as far as the intersection with the GR9, at the D111a.

8Km
2

Junction with the GR9

The GR9 leads to Apt, on the left, and on the right to Saint-Jean-de-Sault. The GR6 drops down to a quarry, goes across it and after having crossed the D111a, borders on the hamlet of Les Gays. Shortly afterwards, go left along a path, pass the crossroads and continue straight ahead.

Detour 30 mins
SAINT-SATURNIN D'APT
At the crossroads, go right uphill to the village.

Soon the GR6 turns right and cuts across the D943, goes along by the camping ground and reaches a surfaced road. Cross the road and shortly afterwards turn left so that on Pérréal hill you can join a broad path which passes near a new villa with a tower.

8Km
2

Detour: *At the new villa, the right-hand road climbs to the top of the hill; from here you get a panoramic view, see traces of a Gallo-Roman* oppidum, *and the chapel of Sainte-Radegonde. To get back to the GR6, take an old path on the right (south), which descends in three loops to the ruins of a* bastide *encircled by cypresses.*

The path goes along the east slope of the hill, offering a view over the Luberon, the plateau of Les Claparèdes, the Apt plain, Les Puits hill, Colorado, Villars and the Albion plateau. It borders the ruins of a *bastide* surrounded by cypresses and descends to fallow land. By-passing the hamlet of Les Tamisiers to the north, and going alongside the D101, you will reach the Gargas crossroads, where you take a small road to the right for 500 metres to reach Gargas itself.

GARGAS
273m

After a crossroads (IGN ref 295), take the road left which enters the woods of La Gardette. As you leave the woods, turn right and go down to a small valley; you will come out on a small road. Go left for 400 metres and then leave the road for the D4; 250 metres further on, facing the Clos d'Urbane farm, go left along a broad path for 30 metres, then leave that, turning left

8Km
2

ROUSSILLON
⌂ ✕ 🚉
350m

10Km
2:30

GORDES
🏠 ⚠ ✕ 🚉 🚌
330m
This district was occupied by
the Celts and Romans.
11th century château,
reconstructed around 1500;
houses with handsome
façades cluster around the
church.

4Km
1

Abbaye de Sénanque
Founded in 1148 by Alphant,
bishop of Cavaillon, and by
the Simianes (Lords of
Gordes), who donated the
land. The abbey, sited at the
bottom of a valley in the wild
plateau of Vaucluse, is one
of the three Cistercian sister-

on to a path which runs beside a farm, up through the arable land and joins the D104 not far from the hamlet of Ferriers. Go right along the D104 for about a kilometre, beside the Colline de Pierroux. When the road heads left (south), go ahead on the cart track which comes out on the D199. Go left down this road for about 250 metres, then turn right on to a sandy path, which leads into the ancient ocre quarries of Roussillon. The footpath becomes narrower and turns into a track that winds up and down before it arrives at Roussillon. Be sure to follow the route-markers here.

In the square, take a street which emerges on to the D169, and follow that downwards for a kilometre. Turn left on a road which leads to Rossignol farm. The path takes a westerly direction, crosses a stream, the Imergue, and then the D60 (IGN ref 189). Continue through the arable land as far as the D2, which you then follow left for 250 metres; turn right along a cart track and, shortly before the hamlet of Les Grailles, turn left to follow a footpath which crosses a road and arrives at the D2 again; a few metres further on, you will find a little street climbing up to the church at Gordes.

The GR crosses the town and after the car park follows the D177 on the route to the abbey of Sénanque and Vénasque; after a bend in the road, take the path on your right leading up to an oratory. At the intersection with the road to Sénanque, you will see what used to be the monks' hostel, which is now a country *gîte*. All the barrow-loads of material for the construction of the abbey were taken along the mule-track which now forms the GR. Follow this ancient path to reach the pass on the Vénasque road, where there is a cross; the path descends into the valley, providing lovely views of the abbey of Sénanque.

The GR crosses the Sénanque road and heads north, crossing the Sénancole and climbing to an oak wood. It passes near the 'Penitent', a single rock standing out from a rocky spur. Then, amidst boxwood, rosemary and broom, the footpath emerges on to the plateau. Continue right, which gives you a view over the Petit Luberon and the Alpilles, then turn left; traverse the Plan plateau, wooded

5Km
1:15

houses of Provence. In 1969 the community left this abbey for the monastery of Saint-Honorat in the Îles de Lérins (off the coast near Cannes). The Society of the Friends of Sénanque has now established a centre for medieval research at the abbey, and a museum of the Sahara.

11Km
2:45

Basse Pouraque
600m
Well preserved ruins; a more modern sheepfold.

10Km
2:30

FONTAINE-DE-VAUCLUSE

The sparkling waters of the Sorgue run through this pleasant village. Fountain (one of the most powerful resurgent streams in the world); Norbert Casteret museum (collections from his cave explorations); ruins of the château of the bishops of Cavaillon.

and stony. You will thus reach La Basse Pouraque.

Go westwards along a stony path, leave it on the right and turn left, then right 80 metres further on. After about 800 metres, descend to the Grande-Combe by a new path. Pass the Oule fountain; sometimes the spring here is dry. The descent becomes more rapid in the Grande-Combe, which widens to form a rocky hollow bordered by high cliffs. You come out on a minor tarmacked road called the 'Chemin de la Vignasse' (115 metres), which you can take to the right to reach Fontaine-de-Vaucluse.

The GR91 emerges here, on its way from Châtillon-en-Diois.

To find the GR6 again, you must return to the crossroads of the Grande-Combe path and the Chemin de la Vignasse. Follow this road straight ahead to La Bastide Rouge (179 metres); before you get to the bridge, turn left on a footpath which goes up a coomb and crosses the forest of Lagnes. Ford a stream and as long as the footpath overlooks the stream, continue on it, leaving on the left a small path which goes off to the next little valley. The GR crosses a plantation of cedars and Aleppo pines. Turning round, you can see the Bondelon shelf, once the site of an *oppidum*, which seems to shut off the coomb. At a crossroads, take the right-hand road which descends (312 metres) as far as the remains of a plague wall, built in 1720 to prevent those with the plague from entering the region. Turn left 500 metres further on, down a cartroad into a pine forest, until you meet the D100.

Detour *15 mins*
LAGNES

You get to the village by following the D100 to the right.

Take the D100 left for about 250 metres, then follow the first road on the right for the next 80 metres (it is not very clearly marked). Then turn left, and at the crossroads in a pinewood turn right, and straightaway right again, descending south to the D147. Go right along that road, which comes out at the N100 by the stop for the Apt-Avignon coaches. Go right along the N100 for about 100 metres, and then take a little surfaced road off on the left, cross the railway line, follow it to the right for 300 metres and then turn left to cross the River Coulon (also called Calvalon). This brings you to the outskirts of Robion.

ROBION
130m

There are traces of neolithic settlement near the Boulon spring in the south of the village. A large number of relics have been found in the neighbouring caves, which seem to have been inhabited until the Roman era.

2Km
0:30

Cross the D2 and go down the avenue of chestnut-trees; turn left on to a stony path which goes along by the cemetery; follow it for 1 kilometre to point 124 on the map, then take the path to the right which emerges at the camping ground at Maubec.

MAUBEC
130m

In the old village, there are sarcophaguses cut into the rock.

Without entering the village, pass the camping ground, and at its entrance follow right, and again right, the Chemin de la Combe de Saint-Pierre, then right once more the Chemin de la Pinière. After turning left, go right, into the Vallon de Pourcéou ('swine'); although the GR does not take you into this valley, it is worth making a detour. Climb left along a path bordered by oak saplings, first on a steep slope, and then more or less horizontal. Cross the scree, going down and then up again. Take a horizontal course, then descend to a clearing which is bordered by a path made specially for the GR; follow this as far as the Bertrand trail, by which you climb to a pass.

4Km
1

Detour. *2 hrs 15 mins on the right, there is a path to the crest of the Luberon, which continues left along the forest route as far as Bastidon-du-Pradon, where you will rejoin the GR6.*

From the pass, go down the footpath without changing direction; climb a little and then come down again to reach a cottage on the left, where you turn right to reach the stony Combrès path. To the right a path marked out in yellow climbs to the little Vallon de Combrès and ends in a cul-de-sac. Turn left instead, and 50 metres on, turn right; at the crossroads take the right-hand path, the old road from

Oppède to Maubec, which rises towards the
D176, which you take to the right in order to
emerge at the square of Oppède-le-Vieux.

OPPÈDE-LE-VIEUX
✗ ▦
297m
*Last place to get water
before Mérindol. The
château and the church
dominate the village, built on
a rocky spur. Old covered
market; town hall in the
square; château, reached by
the path which passes the
chapel of the
Pénitents-Blancs;
Notre-Dame d'Alidon, a
massive 12th and 14th
century construction. From
here you can see the Petit
Luberon to the south; to the
east, the Claparèdes
plateau; to the north, the
mountains of the Vaucluse,
Lure and Ventoux; to the
west, the plain of Avignon
and the Rhône valley.*

5Km
1:30

Detour, *4 hrs.*
*From here you can take a
forest road, marked in yellow,
which rejoins the GR6 at Le
Bastidon-du-Pradon.*

BASTIDON-DU-PRADON
⌂
699m

From the square, take the road to the left with
the fountain, then a quick right, along the road
to the hospital; pass under the vault of the
Hôtel-Dieu and go down a little street as far as
a fortified gate; step through and turn right to
find a footpath dug out of the rock. At a
crossroads, go right along the ancient trail
which climbs to the Massian cross.

The footpath goes up to the right on the
plateau, amid the boxwood. Cross the Hautes-
Plaines forest road; 80 metres further along
you will find Le Bastidon-du-Pradon on the
right.

Continue on the path which crosses the
plateau and follows the ridge of Serre Longue
to the far south. Then you overlook the Vallon
de Roumigué on the right, and that of the
Aigado on the left (sheer and dangerous). The
view extends first to the Vallon de Roque
Rousse, the *craux* of Mayorques and Saint-
Phalès separated by the Gorges de Régalon;
then to the Vallée de la Durance, and further
still, to the Alpilles, La Montagne Sainte-
Victoire and, in the south-east, to the Berre
lake and the sea. From this view point, go to
the right down a marked track which winds
down to the forest road; take the latter to the
left. (This track has been specially devised to
allow the GR6 to descend to the road easily.)
After about 750 metres, leave the road in order

to go down into the valley of La Galère, with its Montpellier maples; when you come out of the valley, take the road on your right which crosses luxuriant vegetation to arrive at the entrance to the Gorges de Régalon.

Detour
The Gorges de Régalon

These gorges were once an underground defile whose roof caved in at the end of the pliocene era, as the sea retreated. There are two caves facing each other in which traces of neolithic settlement have been found. In another, called the 'Dentales' an important funeral hoard was discovered, including necklaces of pearls and teeth, and a flint dagger, which are now on display in the Calvet museum in Avignon. Exploration of the gorges is impracticable in rainy or thundery weather, because of the holes full of water.

14Km
3:30

After leaving the forest road and descending to the valley of La Galère, you will find that the GR6 turns left at the end of the valley; however you should continue straight ahead along the footpath that leads to the defile. You can thus walk along the bottom of the gorges, sometimes between rock faces up to 30 metres high, sometimes clambering over enormous rocks; in parts, the gorge is scarcely a metre wide. You go under a tunnel, and shortly afterwards, under a mass of rock, and soon leave the gorges behind you.

The GR takes a path to the left which comes out on the Crau de Saint-Phalès (if this path along the upper part of the gorges is not usable you should return to the valley of La Galère and continue along the forest road, which ends at Saint-Phalès).

The footpath winds between high cliffs along a dark, narrow passage, but soon it opens out below the forest road, which it rejoins. Go to the right; after the Saint-Phalès farm, turn right, then 50 metres further on turn left (east). Carry on by a footpath which crosses a grassy area, then descend into a gully among tall broom and Aleppo pines. At the end of the little valley there is a dam, built to hold the water from streams on the plain. The GR once again joins the forest road which descends on the right; where it forks, turn left on to a road which climbs to the forest. This is the former boundary between the Comtat Venaissin and Provence. Emerging from the woods, go right on the Chemin des Plaines. You will pass the farms of Meynard and Sadaillan. Where the roads intersect, continue in the same direction; ignore a road on your right and a small valley, but immediately after that go right, up a footpath. This makes its way through the reafforestation on the Peyre-Plate plateau; it is difficult to follow, so observe the markings carefully. There are views of the Durance valley and the Luberon to the north. At the edge of the plateau, take the footpath heading

right (south-west), down to a stand of Aleppo pines and as far as a private estate; then take the Lapied road (on the left, a stony path goes down directly to Mérindol) upwards to Vieux-Mérindol.

Vieux-Mérindol
194m
The village was destroyed in 1545, after the massacre of the inhabitants, by order of the Parliament of Aix, to stamp out the Waldensian heresy.

1Km
0:15

The GR goes down a pebbly path as far as a small surfaced road; go left along that behind the village. By a little street you enter Mérindol.

MÉRINDOL
160m

5Km
1:05

Facing the church, the GR turns left, then right along the road to the fountain as far as the D973, which it crosses. At La Bourdille, take the westernmost road on the right, passing by a washing-place (where there is drinking water). Opposite that, take the path to the right which goes along the foot of the Fontaine des Amoureux and comes out at a surfaced road. Follow this in the same direction, turn left along the D116, then right. Go under the railway bridge and continue on, turning right to the Mallemort road (D23a). Go left on that, cross the River Durance and then the Alpilles canal to arrive at Mallemort.

MALLEMORT
114m
The village is situated on the bank of the Durance. It has a Templars' keep from the 15th century, also an Electricité de France hydro-electrics installation. Melons are a speciality of the village.

2Km
0:30

Leave the village by the D23c in the direction of Charleval. You cross a broad canal and arrive at a crossroads.

Detour *20 mins*
DOMAINE DE VERGON
Continue along the D23c at the crossroads.

At the crossroads, take the little-used road on your right (the D17a), which meets up with the N7 at Vielle-Poste.

Vielle-Poste
145m
Detour *10 mins*
hamlet of
PONT-ROYAL

1Km
0:15

The GR crosses the N7 and takes the D17a slightly off to the right, in the direction of Alleins. One kilometre further on, take a dirt track on the left, which crosses a canal over a little bridge.

Continue west for 500
metres along the N7.

Canal
Detour 30 mins
ALLEINS

Continue straight along the
D17a.
A very picturesque village,
with remains of the old 14th
century village still visible.
Ruins of 16th century
château; 17th century belfry;
Penitents' church;
Renaissance house;
cemetery with Roman chapel
incorporating fragments of
sculpture from the temple at
Vernègues.

4Km
1:30

Keep following this road; in the south it
crosses the *garrigue* (scrubland), then turns
west, skirting a large meadow; it narrows and
rises towards the country in the south-east,
amidst the *restanques*, terraced slopes, oaks,
pines and broom it comes to a small plateau,
where there is a dried-up fountain and a
drinking trough. The path becomes a road
through arable land and climbs a little valley
(with a spring), which is relatively sheltered
from the cold winds. It comes out at the ruins
of the former village of Vieux-Vernègues.

Vieux-Vernègues
350m
Destroyed by an earthquake
in 1909.

Detour: in the north-west, at
the far edge of a huge
plateau (391 metres), there
is a viewpoint with a
panoramic map, and views
over the Alpilles, the
Durance and the Petit
Luberon. There are also
prehistoric dwellings carved
out of the tufa rock, and
tombs.

1Km
0:20

You will see the road below on the left, leading
to the new village; ignore that and continue
west on a dirt track to meet the D22d, which
you follow to the right as far as the intersection
with the D16.

D16
259m
The ruins of the Chapelle de
Saint-Jean are several
metres north.

5Km
1:15

Take the road opposite which crosses a field
in a southerly direction. At a crossroads, not
far from the chapel of Saint-Martin, take the
little road to your right (south-west), then a few
metres further on, go left up a dirt track across
woods and skirt Le Petit Bosquet. The GR
leaves this road and by a little path descends
to a clearing where there is a broad road
leading on the right to the Petit Sonailler farm.
Take this road left the length of a wall (where
there are vines); it crosses the wood of Le
Grand Bosquet and arrives at a wide forest
track, used for riding. Take this to the right

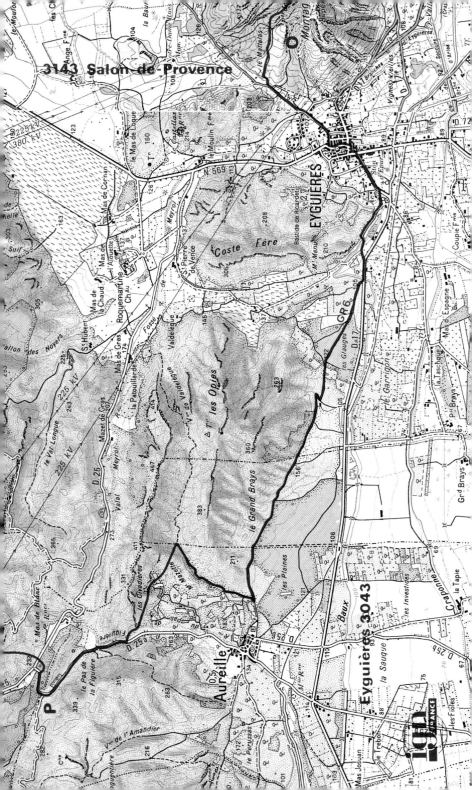

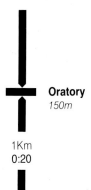

Oratory
150m

1Km
0:20

Pas de l'Ane
220m

1Km
0:20

Roquerousse
160m

1Km
0:15

Roquerousse electricity station
140m

5Km
1:15

Gare de Lamanon
110m

1Km
0:15

LAMANON

The village is situated at the foot of Montagne du Défens, the furthest eastern foothill of the Alpilles.
12th century church; ruins of 12th century chapel of Saint-Jean; 17th century Panisse Château and park; 17th century parish church of Saint-Denis; a listed plane tree 6 metres in diameter.

1Km
0:15

(west); it rises above the little valley of Le Sauvage, and there is a good view of the dolomitic site of Roque-Rousse. In two large loops it descends to the gully at Tallagard in the south, near an oratory.

The GR takes a right turn down an alley of great pines to cross an orchard and grassy ground. **Warning**: when the path comes to the edge of a wood and becomes rugged as it rises, the GR leaves it for a little path on the right, across the *garrigue* northwards to meet a rocky ridge, then winds down a small valley to reach the Pas de l'Ane (Donkey Pass).

Cross an area of scrubland to find a cart track at the edge of a wood; this leads to the Roquerousse farm.

These are arable lands once more, and you will soon arrive at the electricity station at Roquerousse.

Take the little surfaced road to the right (north), keeping the motorway on your left, skirt the Aire de Repos de Lamanon. When you reach the airforce barracks (now an old people's home), turn left (west) to cross the motorway, the EDF (*Electricité de France*) canal, and the N538. You will arrive at the level crossing and Gare de Lamanon (station).

The GR follows the D17d, lined with plane-trees, in a south-westerly direction alongside a playing field, then an esplanade, and turns right to arrive in Lamanon.

To the left of the church take a road which climbs up to a pine wood, then the big shallow steps which become a cobbled ramp before reaching the Grottes des Calès.

Grottes de Calès (Calès Caves)

208m

Excavations have shown that these were inhabited from the neolithic era then, with ingeniously added amenities such as partitions, stairs, furniture, and gutters to take water to cisterns, up to the 15th century. To visit these caves, go under a porch leading to an elliptically-shaped plateau. This is situated between two cliffs, linked by high walls with doors cut into them. Above the caves is the ruin of a Saracen tower.

4Km
1

Signpost for

Le Défends

311m

Beautiful view of the Crau Plain and the Alpilles.

3Km
0:45

EYGUIÈRES

107m

This village is at the gate to the Alpilles.

Oratories; fountains; Romanesque chapel of Saint-Véridèmes behind the cemetery.

7Km
1:45

AUREILLE

117m

9Km
2:30

If you follow the path northwards leading to the Romanesque chapel of Saint-Denis, after five minutes' walk you will find a bountiful spring. The GR goes up between rocks worn by erosion and others which have been hewn out, to give a view over the plateau. It skirts to the north the rocky mound on top of which stands a statue of the Madonna, then goes down a long flight of steps cut into the sandstone and penetrates the undergrowth amidst dense vegetation. When the path goes downwards to the south, take another one on the right (north-west) which goes up to the *garrigue* (watch out for the route-markers, there are a lot of paths) to meet a wide forest path (220 metres). Proceed uphill on this path but before you reach the top, turn left on a path that goes westward and takes you to the edge of the rocky ridge and the signpost for Le Défends.

Continue on this path, which descends a steep slope northwards as far as a forest track. Take this track to the left to meet the D72, and follow that left as far as Eyguières.

The GR crosses the village and takes the D17 in the direction of Mouriès; when you reach the cemetery, take the road on the right which runs along by a canal then crosses it to gain the D17 once more. After crossing the canal, follow it to the right for 200 metres, then take a path on the right, parallel to the road, which winds among almond-trees, pines and scrubland and leads to Aureille.

The GR does not go through the village; 500 metres before it, it turns right (north) on to a track suitable for vehicles which skirts Mont Mazette (224 metres). One kilometre further on, go left up a very steep path in the direction of La Balme de Larron, amongst pines, rocks and orchards. The GR crosses a stream and meets the D25a.

Take the D25a to the right for 2 kilometres; before the crossroads with the D25. To the right of IGN ref 232 cross a little wood, and then the D25. The GR heads along a forest path which rises to the west of the Alpilles chain, then drops to the north-west on a slope of Le Gros Calan ridge. One kilometre further

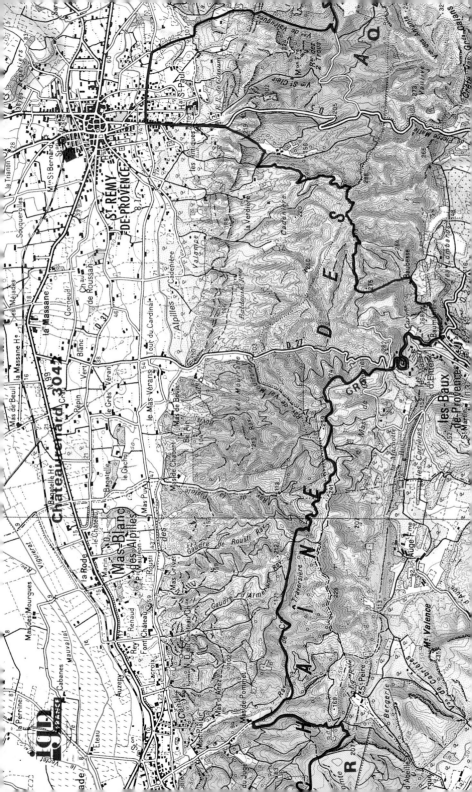

on, ignore the road to the left and continue north on a path which goes along little gorges; skirt a quarry, then cross the D24b to reach Eygalières.

EYGALIÈRES

Ⓗ ⌂ ⚓

112m

Little village built in tiers on the hillside, at the foot of a ruined castle-keep; famous for its corn mills and windmills.

Detour: *If you follow the D24b east for a kilometre, you will arrive at the chapel of Saint-Sixte, built in the 12th century; the first hermit went to live there in 1729, the last one died there in 1855. In Roman times an important spring rose here, and its waters were chanelled along an aqueduct to Arles.*

5Km
1:15

The GR leaves the village and travels west, passing the cemetery to the north. Again it crosses the D24b, and having run along by the Mas de Liset, intersects with the D24 at Cordeliers, where there is a little Roman bridge. Take the *chemin carrossable* which follows the line of the rocky ridge and then, among pines, reaches the Mas de Romanin.

Mas de Romanin

120m

Ruins of the château de Romanin, where there was a Cour d'Amour (Court of Love) in the 14th century.

1.5Km
0:45

Walk along the boundary of the estate as far as the Alpilles gliding school.

The GR goes south beside the gliding school, then along the waste ground as far as the edge of the wood; at that point, it plunges into a little valley where it climbs over the scree then goes through a narrow gully which leads between oak and boxwood to the Vallongue pass.

Col de Vallongue

354m

This was the route taken by the troubadours when they went to the Château de Romanin. It is difficult to keep your balance on this pass when the mistral blows.

5Km
1:30

The GR goes along the south slope of the Alpilles (follow the markings carefully when crossing the small screes), threads its way between the rocks amidst rosemary, scrub-oaks and cistus, to reach the crest of the Alpilles, from which there is a good view over the plain and the gliding school. Follow the ridges westwards, crossing some rocky sections, to reach a little plateau from which you can see a television relay station. Guided by little cairns of stone and keeping in the same direction, you will come to the signpost for La Caume.

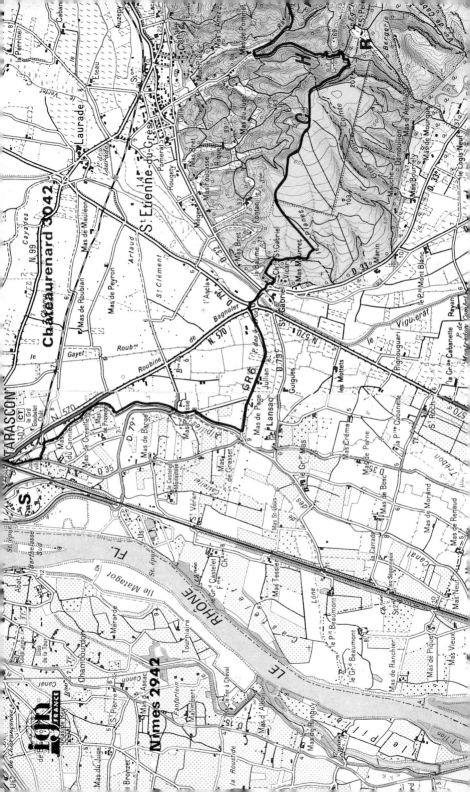

Signal de la Caume
391m
Highest point of the western Alpilles, offering a wide panorama.

6Km
1:30

SAINT-RÉMY-DE-PROVENCE

79m
small town at foot of Alpilles. Ruins of Roman city, Glanum; Les Antiques (mausoleum and arch); monastery of Saint-Paul-du-Mausolée.

2Km
0:45

Lac de Saint-Rémy
170m
A small artificial lake.

6Km
1:30

LES BAUX-DE-PROVENCE

210m
Village on a rocky spur at the west of the Alpilles, a strange conglomeration of rock eroded by the wind. Ruins of a spectacular château, the scene of many battles. Famous from the 11th to the 17th centuries but razed in 1632 on the orders of Louis XIII. This

9Km
2:30

Crossing the plateau in a south-westerly direction, the GR arrives at the road servicing the television relay station situated 300 metres south; go down it for a kilometre, then turn right on to a road which first of all threads through the densely wooded Vallon de Valrugues, then through orchards and olive-groves until it reaches the Provence canal and the D5, 500 metres away from Saint-Rémy-de-Provence.

The GR follows the D25 which leads to Les Antiques and Glanum; 500 metres after Les Antiques, turn to the right on a footpath which twists through the pines and then up a steep slope to reach a crest where a chimney in the rock — naturally formed, and now well kept — permits a descent by metal ladders to a footpath, from which you will discover the lake of Saint-Rémy spread out below.

Go round the south side of this lake, cross the stream which feeds it and climb straight ahead, among handsome fir-trees, as far as a road. Cross this in order to reach a forest path going south. This passes between two rocks and comes out at a road along the ridges (309 metres). Follow this road westward for 1.3 kilometres (to IGN ref 275). Turn left there, and descend a small valley (south) which is a bare wilderness, until you reach Baubesse, a beautiful house. Take a road on the right which leads to disused underground quarries. This becomes a footpath between rocks, and leads to Les Baux-de-Provence.

The GR does not go through the village: when it reaches the car park in the Baumanière area, it takes the D27 to the right for 2 kilometres. The road crosses the Val d'Enfer (Hell Valley), providing a fine vista over Les Baux, and the GR cuts across its last bend.

exceptional site is world famous and offers a grand panoramic view.

Detour, *2.5 Kilometres*
'LA GROTTE NOIR'
⌂

Detour, see left. From the pass you can leave the GR and walk for 2.5 kilometres due west, to reach the hostel for riders, 'La Grotte Noire'.

At the pass, go north, taking a road on your left which roughly follows the ridges (273 metres), then veer west to descend, after several kilometres, to the Traversière ravine and gain the Mas de Pommet.

Mas de Pommet
66m

Detour
SAINTE-ETIENNE-DU-GRÈS
Å 🚂 🚌
A little road leads to this area from the mas.

6Km
1:30

The GR goes left along a road that rises southwards, in a beautiful wooded valley. Proceed as far as the crossroads, where there is a cluster of houses, and there turn right (west) in the direction of the crests of Le Planet. Three kilometres further on, turn to the right along a forest path and, where it widens, take the path on the left which descends to the Chapelle Saint-Gabriel.

CHAPELLE
SAINT-GABRIEL
Å ✕
15m
12th century Romanesque chapel, with a finely sculpted façade. At this point you have reached the extreme west of the Alpilles chain. Here the limestone, rosemary and thyme, pines and oaks give way to the plain and the rice fields, beyond which rise the imposing towers of Tarascon.

6Km
1:30

At the crossroads, take the road in the direction of Tarascon. Fifty metres further on, go left along the D35 for 1.4 kilometres, as far as the Alpines canal. Take the right-hand path which runs beside the canal as far as the entrance to Tarascon.

TARASCON
🏠 ✕ 🚂 🚐 🚌
Tarascon is a small town on the left bank of the Rhône, dominated by the beautiful church of Saint-Marthe and the great mass of its castle, which faces the rock and castle of Beaucaire on the right bank, defending the entry to Languedoc.

The GR6 continues in the *département* of the Gard in the direction of Mont Aigoual.

WALK 4

BRANTES
⌂ ✗ ⚓

600m

Gîte 2 km away (Fontaube farm).

3:45

Abri du Contrat
1200m

0:20

Detour 20 mins
MONT SEREIN RESORT
⌂ ✗

Follow the road west for 1500 metres.

Separation of the
GR4 and the GR9.

1:30

The GR9 runs south, past the grocery/inn and the war memorial. It goes through a gate, descends a stairway to the left and, along a grassy footpath, reaches the D40 (where there is a bus shelter). Go right along this road for several metres, then turn left on to the D164a. Pass through La Frache. When you reach the last house in Les Grandes de Bernard, go left up a narrow tarred road. The GR climbs south between low, crumbling drystone walls, and passes a water tower. Further up, go left along the forest path (not surfaced); at the first fork, ignore the Savoillans road on the left; the GR proceeds west on the forest path, fords a stream and passes a foresters' shelter on the left. Leave the forest path 1.5 kilometres further on, and turn sharp left on to a footpath. The GR twists and turns through a dense forest, providing views over the Bois Marou and the rocky escarpment of Grave Faouletière. At the road, go left to reach the shelter at Le Contrat.

Here you will come across the GR4, coming from the summit of Mont Ventoux. It goes off to the north-west, along the shelf ending the surfaced road to the Col du Comte.

The two GRs reach the forest path, leaving a drainage ditch on the right; at the first bend of the forest path, they separate.

The GR4 continues on the forest path, which twists upwards towards the summit of Mont Ventoux. The GR9 continues along the north face of Mont Ventoux.

Walkers may take either the GR4 or the GR9 to reach the hut at La Frache.
On the following pages, the GR4 itinerary is described as far as the hut at La Frache, where it meets the GR9 again.

Alternative route: GR4 from Le Contrat to the cabin at La Frache. This route goes via the summit of Mont Ventoux.

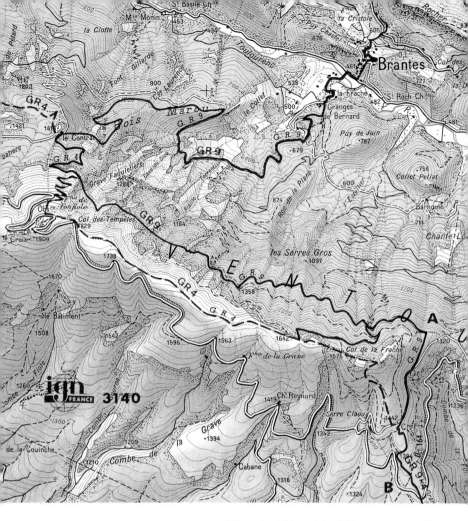

When the GR4 and the GR9 separate, the GR4 takes the forest path, which continues to twist upwards; you will pass near the Font-Fiole spring, where there are alpine flowers, and reach the summit of Mont Ventoux.

MONT VENTOUX

✗ ♟

1912m
Military observatory; air force radar station. An immense panorama.

The climb up Mont Ventoux or rather, the 'Ventour' via the Pas Forest and the ridge, offer already extensive views. *From the summit, to the north*: there are the mountains of La Lance, joined by the furthest mountains of the Drôme, in front of which opens the valley of the Ouvèze; further back, between the high valley of the Drôme and that of the Durance, there is the Col de Cabre; then the peaks of the enormous escarpments of the Trièves and the

Dévoluy, between Gap and Grenoble; Obiou, Ferrand, Pic de Bure (the GR94 covers all this region); then the Grand Alps of the Dauphiné; Le Pelvoux, Le Viso; and the deep depression of the Durance between Gap and Manosque. *To the south-east*: the Alpes Maritimes. *To the south*: the Vaucluse mountains, Marseille (you can make out Notre-Dame de la Garde), and the Alpilles. Further still, beyond the Arles plain, the sea appears as a brilliant line on the horizon. *To the south-west*: Montpellier and Nîmes. *To the west*: the Cevennes, and the long ridge of Mont Lozère. *In the north-west*: you can see along the Rhône and the Vivarais mountains, beneath which stand the Mézenc and the Gerbier-de-Jonc.

The GR descends the crest road, which is staked out with iron posts painted red; passes to the north of the first military 'silo', situated on the Col des Tempêtes (Stormy Pass), then continues in the same direction (south-east) as far as an unnamed pass.

1:30

Col Non Dénommé
1600m

Detour
CHALET-REYNARD
Ⓗ

Detour, see left. From this little pass, at the level of the ski-lift, go left along a route marked out in yellow spots, which joins the GR9. Descending to the right on the thalweg for 1 kilometre, you will arrive at the Chalet-Reynard, a hotel with a restaurant.

0:30

The GR4 then reaches a surfaced road, on a corner; to the left you will see a second 'silo', in a forbidden military zone. Cross the road and descend opposite into the forest by the marked footpath, in the general direction of the south-east as far as a crossroads.

Crossroads
1442m
This is near a dilapidated wooden hut called the 'Cabane de la Frache'. It is the junction with the GR9, which arrives opposite, having traversed the north face of the Ventoux.

Turn right (south); a few metres further on you pass the La Frache hut.

1:30

This route provides fine views of the Toulorenc valley and the Drôme mountains.

When the GR9 and the GR4 separate, the GR9 continues south-east along a cliff road on the north slope of Mont Ventoux. The path crosses the Faouletière gullies and goes through an ancient natural forest. You will find a path marked out in yellow.

Path marked out in yellow

1

Taking this path to the right, you will rejoin the GR4 on the crest of Mont Ventoux. The GR9 bends twice and passes near the ruined Serre-Gros hut (1350 metres), and reaches the escarpment of La Frache.

Epaulement de la Frache
1400m
There are beehives in the meadow, which are very dangerous in thundery weather. Extensive views over the Vercors range and the Pelvoux massif.

0:30

Continue to the right, along the forest path; where it splits into three, keep on the right. Further on you will reach a crossroads.

Crossroads
1442m
This is near a dilapidated wooden hut called the 'Cabane de la Frache'.

0:30

The GR4 emerges opposite, coming from the top of Le Ventoux via the crest. From the crossroads the GR9 and the GR4 follow the same route as far as Jas Forest. Thus at the crossroads the GR9 turns left (south); a few metres further on, it passes the La Frache hut. The two GRs continue south and cross the D164, where there is a belvedere. Still going south, on a wide road across a plateau with woods of black pines and Scotch firs, they arrive at a crossroads, which is the junction with the GR91b.

Junction with the GR91b
Known as the 'Sentier des Bergeries' (Sheepfolds' Way), this is the only cross country path on the south face of the Ventoux, at an average altitude of 1000 metres.

0:40

The two GRs continue south to a wide path, which they take to the left as far as the forest hut of the Jas Forest.

Jas Forest
1131m
Here the GR9 and the GR4 separate; the GR4 heads towards Sault-de-Vaucluse. Hikers can take the GR4 via Verdolier and Sault, rejoining the GR9 at the Roteau

The GR9 continues southwards along the forest path. After a few kilometres you reach a surfaced road. Go left along it for 80 metres, then go down a forest path on your right. When you arrive opposite the Croix de Fer farm, the GR9 turns on to the right-hand road and joins another road which it follows to the left for 1500 metres. The GR9 then reaches a bend in

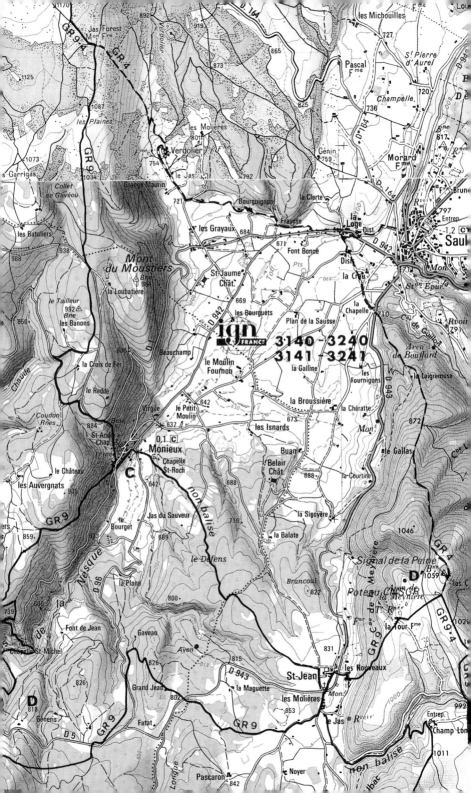

1:30   *CNSGR (map ref D). The description begins below.*

Detour *20 mins*
MONIEUX
✕
600m

Verdolier
754m
A village at the bottom of the Haute-Nesque valley.
18th century church, forming a handsome group with the washing-place and fountain.

0:45

Stream
671m
Detour *30 mins*
SAULT
🏠 ⛺ ✕ 🚋 🚌
780m
Once you have crossed the stream, turn left to follow a path then a little route marked in orange, as far as the transformer situated below the town.

1

the road, and takes a footpath through the wood on the right: be very careful to follow the markings here, as there are many little paths. Descend the Saint-André coomb, and you will reach a clear space at the foot of the ruins of the Château de Monieux, where the rocks overlook the village. The GR then turns right and crosses the coomb, remaining on the hillside; it heads towards the Gorges de la Nesque.

Go down to the left over the rocks, and follow very old markings in red and blue.

Alternative route from Monieux to Saint-Jean. Walkers going down to Monieux may take a route devised by F. Morénas which avoids the Gorges de la Nesque, or enables you to walk round it joining up with the GR9. It rejoins the GR9 at Saint-Jean; this route is marked on the map but is not waymarked.

Alternative route GR4 from the Jas Forest to the CNSGR post (1037 metres). From the Jas Forest hut, the GR4 goes left and descends a steep slope in a south-easterly direction to reach the hamlet of Verdolier.

Take the surfaced road south-east for 1 kilometre, then turn left along a road shared by the GR and a riding track, marked in orange. You will pass the Auberge de Bourguignon (accommodation available), and reach the D942 by a path. Follow the road to the left as far as the first house of the hamlet of La Loge. The GR4 leaves the road here for a path to the left (south), crossing the stream on stones.

Once it has crossed the stream, the GR4 continues opposite along a path which cuts across several minor roads and comes out at a round building situated at the edge of the D943. Cross the road to reach a path nearly opposite, which is steep and rocky but becomes easier as it reaches an area wooded with pines, oaks and beeches. The vegetation gets thinner and you will see the farm and the Signal de La Peine (1057 metres).

*From the Signal, there are
extensive views over the
plateau of Albion, the Lure
mountain and the Pre-Alps
to the east, the Lubéron
range to the south, the
Dentelles de Montmirail and
Mont Ventoux to the west,
and Le Dévoluy.*

Proceed south across the land where *lavandin* (a cross between lavender and aspic, used in the perfume industry) is cultivated, to reach a crossroads.

Crossroads
1037m
*Marked by a CNSGR post.
The junction with the GR9
coming from Saint-Jean.*

0:40

At the fork below Monieux (see page 00), the GR9, crossing the coomb, takes the old cliff road which allows you to admire the view of Monieux, clinging to the side of the mountain, and the plain which extends as far as Sault; 1500 metres further on, leave this road at the level of the hamlet of Flaoussiers (IGN ref 859), and turn left (south) on to a path between oak trees. Arriving at the D942, follow the road right for several metres, then take a footpath which descends steeply. **Warning**: Be especially careful here as parts of the footpath are overhanging. The path comes out at the Chapelle Saint Michael.

Chapelle Saint-Michael
600m
*Built in 1643 under a rocky
overhang forming three
storeys; the first two were
inhabited in prehistoric
times.*

Detour: in 4 hours it is possible to complete a circular walk which goes up northwards, along the ancient muletrack by the stream, the Nesque, as far as Monieux; it then takes the GR9 which re-emerges at the chapel of Saint Michael. It is also possible to leave either from Monieux, or from the intersection of the GR9 with the D942.

Ford the Nesque and turn left. After a twist, the GR goes along the foot of the cliff, and winds through the gorges, which are always cool in summer, and bear traces of prehistoric habitation — bivouac. It arrives at a shelf and then rises to the left through a little gully to attain a plateau. It then passes near the ruins of Le Crémat (not marked on map) and proceeds south-east. Turn right to cross a valley; at a fork, go down the right-hand road (the left gives access to the Poulissen farm) and a little further on, go right again to cross a gully. On the other side, go along the bottom of a valley which leads to the north of the Champ de Sicaude (private property). The GR crosses a scree, then makes a great loop, first heading north and then south-west. After an intersection, where the path veers right, continue

1:30

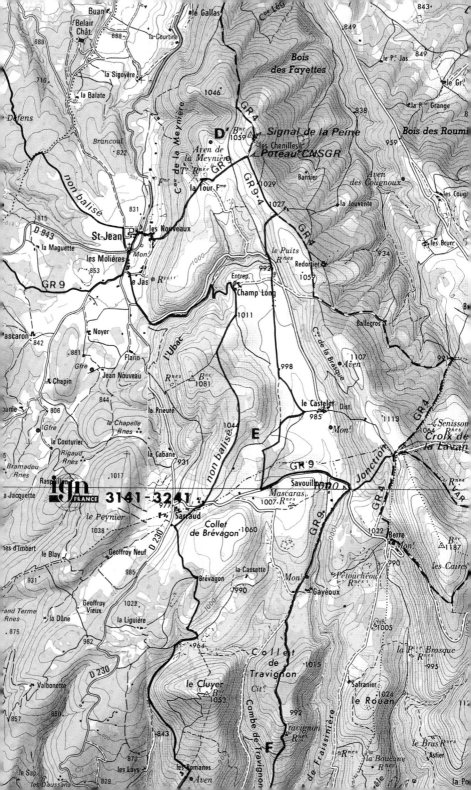

straight ahead. At the next intersection (north of 814 on the map), go left along a path heading south.

Detour *20 mins there and back*
Belvedere
for the Nesque gorges.
Warning: *sheer cliff! By going north you can reach the belvedere above the canyon of the Nesque. It offers striking views of the Gorges de la Nesque and the Rocher du Cire.*

At a junction, near a cedar, go left and several metres further on, turn right on to a footpath on a hillside which overlooks the valley of Champ de Sicaude. Take the first road to your left, then the Méthamis road (sandy and suitable for vehicles), again to the left to end up at the D5. Follow this for 200 metres to the left, to reach the Ferme Saint-Hubert.

Ferme Saint-Hubert
833m

Here there is a junction with the GR91a, which enables you to reach Méthamis in 2½ hours.

2:30

Set off in an easterly direction on the old road from Saint-Hubert to Monieux, which offers views of the Sault plain, the Nesque coomb, Mont Ventoux, the Dentelles de Montmirail and, in the distance, the foothills of the Cévennes. Cross the D5, pass below the farm of La Devendoure (not marked on map) to reach the D96. Take the path opposite, which twists upwards to pass the farm of Champ d'Anguiran (not marked on map), then intersects with the D943. Take the surfaced road to the left, as far as a large boundary stone with directions. Go left here, along the Chemin des Courtois which leads to Saint-Jean-de-Sault.

SAINT-JEAN-DE-SAULT
⌂
800m
The detour path from Monieux appears here.

If you follow this path, you can get to Saint-Saturnin-d'Apt. For a description of the route, see below. The GR9 continues on page 00.

Alternative route (2 hours) via Saint-Saturnin-d'Apt. From Saint-Jean-de-Sault the path is marked out sporadically in yellow (see the lines on the maps for these pages).

This route goes along many private pathways, threads between fields of lavandin *or grain, and passes by houses restored by people who enjoy solitude — so please be unobtrusive, and refrain from picking lavender and mushrooms.*

1:30

Near the washing-place, take a dirt track for 1 kilometre, then go left along the wild, desert-like coomb known as the Ravin de Combe Crau, or simply as Champ Long (it is the access road to the farm of that name); the markings all along the bottom of the ravine follow an ancient dirt track. Pass Champ Long, a stately farm surrounded by enormous chestnut trees, then follow the line of the crest of the

Sarraud plateau, covered in fields of *lavandin*.

Sarraud
977m

The markings, in a southerly direction and at an altitude of 1000 metres, take the hiker across the hills. You skirt the 'collet' of Brévagnon, pass the Barralier 'aiguiers' ('pitchers': the water is not for drinking) and, at Les Romanes (under restoration), the large 'aiguiers' of drinking water (these are private). You then come out below the Combe du Château. The route allows for a long and splendid descent, with the Luberon as back-drop; there are magnificent views of the roofs, with their old Provençal tiles, the dam, the château, the mills, the bell-tower and the remains of the Saracen ruins at Saint-Saturnin-d'Apt.

SAINT-SATURNIN-D'APT
456m

To return to the GR9, take the GR6 east at the campsite, south of the town.

The GR9 goes east from Saint-Jean and crosses the D493. At the hamlet of Les Nouveaux, it heads north-east and, climbing a steep slope, reaches the top of the Côte de la Meynière, from which there is a fine view of the Sault plain and Mont Ventoux. Keep climbing in the same direction; you will pass the farm at La Tour and then reach a crossroads marked by a CNSGR post.

Crossroads
1037m
This is the junction with the GR4 from Sault via the Signal de la Peine.

The GR9 and the GR4 share a path going south-south-east; 800 metres further on, the two GRs separate. The GR4 continues straight ahead, while the GR9 turns right (west), along a row of old trees, and descends to a road (992 on the map). Cross the road and climb a tarmacked road; there is a water-hole in the meadow on the left. You will arrive at a crossroads; on the right there is an access road to the Champ Long. The GR continues straight ahead along a beautiful alley of chestnut trees; there are fields of *lavendin* on the plateau. One kilometre further on (998 on the map) the road first turns left (the path has disappeared on the right), then turns right to resume its initial direction. Arriving at a big crossroads, keep going south on the path upwards; on the brow of the hill, turn right, and go down as far as the road from Sarraud to Savouillon. If you are walking in the opposite direction it looks as though the road is a

2

0:45

1:45

private one, and you can see the remains of a chain preventing entry, but take no notice. Follow the road to the left; after the entrance to the Savouillon farm, you will arrive at a crossroads.

The GR9 leaves the road, turning right (south-east) on a dirt track which it follows as far as the Aiguiers de Gayéoux, to the left of the track. The GR9 continues south; at the first crossroads, where there is a cement water tank, take the left fork along the footpath which climbs up to the ruined hamlet of Travignon (map ref F).

Crossroads

1000m

Here you are very near the GR4, which you can rejoin by a path to your left, mounting north-east.

1:15

TRAVIGNON
⌂
932m

At the foot of Travignon, the GR9 goes down the road on the right which becomes a footpath; at the fourth bend you will pass a path off to the right, and after the next bend, descend directly south as far as the Portes de Castor. The descent proceeds along a farm track; 100 metres before the D179, turn left to pass the Ferme des Noyers.

2

On the left is the ancient Chemin du Dauphiné, also called the Route du Sel (the salt road), well used up to the beginning of the 17th century. It was a wide track that went the length of the Jabron valley to the Calavon valley, and reached the Berre lake in the south via the Loumarin coomb and the Trévaresse.

After the Ferme des Noyers, turn right to meet the D179; cross it and continue along the road opposite (D111a). There is an intersection with the GR6 600 metres further on.

Intersection with the GR6
Detour *45 mins*
SAINT-SATURNIN
ⓗ ▲ ✕ ⛲ 🚌

Detour, see left. Follow the GR6 westwards (right); when the GR6 veers left (south), continue straight ahead on a path which climbs gently up to the village.

1

From the intersection, the GR9 continues along the road for several metres, then turns left on to a road which meets the D214; cross this to reach an oratory (219 metres) a little further on. The GR9 keeps going south, descends, crosses a bridge (there is a water purification plant on the right), rises gently, turns right, then 100 metres on turns left. As it climbs, it passes Saint-Pilibert (where there is water), Le Jas (site of an old still), and Bel-Air. It goes along the Colline des Puits and, at the level of the water tower, begins its descent south. On the left you will see a *borie* (drystone hut). A little later, opposite a hundred-year-old oak, you will find a farm inhabited by an artisan. Pass beneath a high-tension wire (map ref G).

High-tension wire
403m
G on the map.

After passing beneath the wire, proceed downwards. A dirt track cuts across a bend in the road and you come out on the cité Saint-Michel bypass. Take the Rue Jean Mermoz to the right, and then go left on the Avenue Normandie-Niémen, and left again on an

0:45

APT
🏠 ✗ 0 🚌
200m
This ancient town is situated
on the left bank of the
Coulon, a tributary of the
Durance, in a valley
surrounded by hills covered
in olive and fruit trees.
Ancient cathedral of Saint-

unnamed passage ending up at the Avenue Saint-Michel. Take this to the left, and at the chapel of Notre-Dame de la Garde, go down the steps leading to the Avenue de la Garde. Go down the Passage du Lierre which begins with steps and makes an S to arrive at the Avenue Viton; turn right along the avenue (from the opposite direction, the first passage after the bridge), pass beneath the railway bridge and continue to the bridge over the River Coulon. The marking stops at the Route de Rustrel. Cross the bridge to enter the town of Apt.

You will reach the GR9 markings again past the Apt *gendarmerie* (police station), which you will find on the Avenue des Bories. About 200 metres after the *gendarmerie*, go left up the surfaced Chemin de Saint-Massian, as far as the D113; cross that, and go down to the Maurangne stream. After the bridge, go left (south-east) along a dirt track, which becomes a footpath and leads to the Château des Tourrettes. Walk along by the retaining wall,

Anne, recast Romanesque;
crypts, one
pre-Romanesque, the other
Romanesque; 16th century
clock-tower.
Departure point for the GR92,
which goes south to the Étang
de la Bonde (Walk 5).

Chapelle de Clermon

Private, Romanesque
chapel. At the intersection, a
stone marks the boundary
between the ancient Comtat
Venaisson (enclave de
Bonnieux) and the Comté de
Provence. The former priory,
now belonging to Regain,
can operate as a hostel for
walkers. (Write to Regain,
Saignon par 84400 Apt.)

All the way along the
Corniche des Claparèdes —
a walk recommended for June
and July — you overlook the
whole plateau, and see Le
Ventoux, the Vaucluse
mountains and the Alps.

Work began on this château,
built on the remains of a
Roman villa, in the 13th
century, and finished just
before the Revolution.

AUBERGE DE SEGUIN
⌂

then climb left up a goat track; after the intersection with a forest path, follow an excellent tarmacked road as far as the junction with the Chapelle de Clermon.

Alternative route to La Montagne mainly along the roads via Château du Buoux, and the fort.

At Le Ferme du Jas, take the surfaced road south-west which will allow you to see the façade of the Château de Buoux.

The road is lined with great oaks and passes near the priory of Saint-Symphorien (1060, now restored), to reach the D113. Take this to the left to enter the valley of l'Aigue-Brun, with its chaotic heaps of rock indicating prehistoric habitation. At the level of the holiday camp, at the first bend to the left (IGN ref 371), leave the D113 for the road on the right (east), which goes along the cliffs of the Moulin Clos (where people go rock-climbing). In this area, a network of Regain paths enables you to take 2 hour circular walks, or to go round the Aiguille in 5 hours by the Corniche des Ramades. Several hundred metres further on, you will find to the left the access road for the Auberge de Seguin, which offers rooms.

Go to the right along the access road to the ruined Fort de Buoux; it passes enormous caves, used as burial places, and reaches the custodian's house.

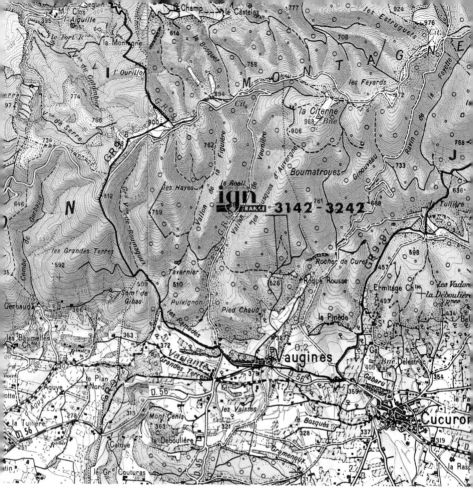

Fort de Buoux

Built in the 12th century on top of an ancient Roman oppidum, the walls of the fort encircled a village and a château. Repaired in the 16th century, it was a stronghold for Protestants until dismantled under Louis XIV.

2

La Montagne
625m

2

Note: At the foot of the fort, two Regain itineraries begin; they go straight across the Montagne du Luberon (marked out by a yellow cross and dots) either via the Gerbaud coomb, and via the Cavaliers coomb, and arrive at Lourmarin in 3 hours.

From the fort, go right for 900 metres, then turn left on to a footpath. When you reach a clearing on your way down, continue to the right. Do not take the footpath descending to the left (private property, no access). You will arrive at a barn called La Montagne.

Take a dirt track from Chapelle de Clermon. Cross the Route des Claparèdes (D232) and, on a surfaced road, you reach Le Jas farm.

Ferme du Jas
444m
*This was the old post house
for stage coaches and carts.
It lies on a continuation of
the salt road which crossed
the Vaucluse mountains.
See opposite page for the
detour to the château and
the Fort de Buoux.*

2

Detour *10 mins*
AUBERGE SEGUIN
Ⓗ ✕
Take the road to the right.

La Montagne
625m
*There is a spring beneath
the buildings.
See opposite page for the
fort and château of Buoux.*

Summit
900m
To the north: *Le Ventoux,
the Lure mountain and the
Pre-Alps.* To the south:
*Saint-Baume,
Sainte-Victoire, the Berre
lagoon, La Crau and the
Mediterranean.*

2:30

The GR goes left, off the surfaced road, to meet the outer wall of the Château de Buoux, and runs along beside it. Go up the path on the right to the plateau. Follow the electricity line along the length of a field, then cut across a road; continue on a dirt track, which gives way to a rocky path descending to the village of Buoux. Take the right-hand road in the direction of the *mairie*. At the transformer, turn right then, 500 metres further on, right again. The road rises quite steeply past houses (please do not make a lot of noise). Turn left on a path that climbs to Marrenon. Steer clear of the farm: go along a road and then down a rocky road, cross the Aigue-Brun and continue to the crossroads.

The GR takes the road on the left, then leaves it to climb up a wide road which curves to the east of the barn called La Montagne.

The GR reaches the ruins of L'Ourillon (map ref I) and climbs a winding footpath south-east as far as the summit (900 on the map).

From the summit descend in a south-easterly direction to reach the ridge road (route des crêtes) near a loop (812). Take this road for 50 metres in the same direction. At the bend climb up an old road to the right as far as the point numbered 898 on the map (the geodesic marker is in ruins). Descend following the ridges, by a road that is difficult to discern at times. You will emerge on the route des crêtes again, near a cement reservoir (not on map). Follow the road in the same direction (south) for 400 metres, and when it turns right (north), take the footpath on the left in a coppice (watch out, as the beginning is not clear). Ignoring some tracks on the right, descend first amidst holm oaks, and then in the open, following the line of the ridge; at the end the slope gets steeper, and the path comes out on a circular road at the foot of the Gibas summit. (Be careful, in the opposite direction, to mark the beginning of the path. The markings between Gibas and the ridges are often rubbed out.) The GR goes left on the circular

road, skirts a ruin on the right, and ignoring first a road on the left then one on the right, curves slightly to the left. Here the path gets wider to serve the houses and becomes a road, intersecting with the road which goes up the valley of Vaumière on the left. Continue eastwards, and shortly afterwards you will find the markings for the GR97, coming from Mérindol. The GRs enter the village of Vaugines together.

Warning: on the outskirts of Vaugines and over most of the Luberon there are wild-pig chases in the hunting season; hikers should take care.

VAUGINES

375m

Commanderie; a 15th

century building, the
Capitainerie; the 12th
century Romanesque
church. There is a fountain
opposite the church. You are
advised to get water here, as
there is no other source until
Vitrolles.

Detour 20 mins
CUCURON
🏠 △ ✕ 🏛
Fossil deposits from the
Neocomian (cretaceous),
Miocene, and Eocene eras.
Follow the D56 for 600
metres.

2:45

Detour
Vitrolles

From Vaugines, you can go straight to the *gîte* at La Rasparine (south-east of Cucuron) by taking the marked alternative route, shown in dashes on the maps on pages 00 and 00.

The GR9 and the GR97, which share the way to Vitrolles, leave Vaugines by going down a little street as far as the church. Go along by an old cemetery, go round it to take a dirt track that ends up at the D56. Take the D56 eastwards; 400 metres further on, turn very sharply left on to a surfaced road, where the GRs head north.

One kilometre further on, go northwards along the bed of a stream; depending on the state of cultivation, you can follow the stream along the right bank. After 600 metres, you will find the common path, much overgrown by crops. It passes the foot and to the west of the hermitage of Notre-Dame de Beauvoir (IGN ref 493). Cross and recross the stream, draw near a ruined farm with a superb chestnut tree beside it, and come out on a pass. Go right, down the forest path from Cucuron to Auribeau. About 300 metres further on, turn left and scramble over some scree to reach a path (dug up in parts) along the edge of a field, which joins a farm track. Follow this to the left. On your right is the farm of La Tullière. The itinerary proceeds along the Chemin de Coustière, sometimes reduced to a rutted footpath. Near a watering-place for wild boar, the GR crosses the beginning of the Vabre gully (not marked on map), goes down through a plantation of pines. It then comes out on a road coming from the plain and going up the flank of the Luberon. Go to the right (south) down this road; several metres on, turn left on to a footpath which climbs again to arrive at the edge of the Méchant gully (not marked on map). Go down into the gully, climb up again, then follow a track meeting an old path which descends to a pebbled path. Follow that to the left, as far as the forest path by which the GR92 comes from Cabrières-d'Aigues (map ref K).

Detour, Vitrolles, via the Route des Crêtes. See the dotted line on the map (map refs K to L). The route is marked out in yellow. Climb up by the GR92 from (point K) northwards as far

149

as the Route des Crêtes (the peak path), then follow the peak path eastwards. You will have a beautiful view to the north and to the south. After about 2 kilometres you pass the basic shelter offered by the Gros Collet. A bit further on, a little path on the right (south) goes down to meet the GR97 in the gully of the Vaucèdes. Follow the forest path eastwards, leave it to go right, down an open footpath via the Parc de Luberon (not labelled on map). Taking the former 'Chemin d'Apt', you will go south-east in the direction of Vitrolles.

Map ref K
Intersection with the GR92.

Following the GR92 to the right (south) for 3 kilometres, you reach Cabrières-d'Aigues. After the first intersection with the GR92, both GRs take a forest path northwards; 100 metres further on the GR9 and the GR97 turn right (north-east), passing near a water-tank, a sheepfold and another water-tank. The route leads to two ruined sheepfolds, then to another water-tank and arrives at a junction of three paths in the gully called Vaucèdes. To the left, a forest path joins the Route des Crêtes of the Grand Luberon. Continue eastwards for several kilometres, past a cement water-tank, until you reach the Bastide du Bois (private property), which is below you on your right. The route then joins up with the forest path, near Mouret farm. Keep going east on the forest path; this veers right (south) to skirt a knoll, at an unnamed pass (*col non dénommé*).

2:45

Col non dénommé
Detour *30 mins*
PEYPIN-D'AIGUES
Go down to your right.

Leave the forest path at this point and go eastwards down a footpath which follows the bed of a stream for most of the way. Rejoin the forest path and follow it for about 100 metres; here, the GRs turn left (north). If you follow the path to the right (south), you will meet the D42 which goes to Peypin-d'Aigues. The GRs climb up towards the Parties gully (not labelled on map). At the edge of it, take the footpath to the right which crosses it, goes along by a ruin (Les Grands Collets), then arrives at a cross-roads in the open. Here, go down left (east) as far as the D33 (Vitrolles–Grambois), and take that road east; you will pass a cemetery, and shortly afterwards the GR9 continues straight on, crosses a stream and climbs up to Vitrolles.

1:30

Vitrolles
This village nestles in the heart of the Luberon.

The GR9 takes the D216 southwards out of Vitrolles, and follows it for 1500 metres; then it turns left on to a footpath, at first level and then descending to the south across woods as far as the ruins of La Tullière, where it rejoins the D216. Follow this to the left, cross the stream of Saint-Pancrace, then go along the left bank for 600 metres. Below the Chapelle Saint-Pierre, turn right on to a footpath which spans the river and comes out on the D42 (Peypin-d'Aigues–La Bastide-des-Jourdans); cross this to reach the hamlet of Fléraque, 800 metres further south. At the entrance to this hamlet, the GR turns sharp right (west) on to a footpath that leads to the Chapelle Saint-Pancrace.

2:30

This chapel, like the family graveyard next to it, belongs to the Château de Pradine. The owner has given permission for walkers to pass through the area; please be unobtrusive and respect the peaceful atmosphere of these places.

From the chapel, the GR9 heads south to reach the D33, which it takes southwards. Further on, it comes out on the N556.

Detour *5 mins*
HOSTELLERIE DES TILLEULS (LIME-TREES)
🏠 ✕
Follow the N556 to the right for 400 metres.

The GR crosses the N556 and takes the footbridge over the Lèze. If there is flooding, this route is not practicable: take the N556 to the left, then the D122 again to the left. The GR climbs to the village of Grambois.

GRAMBOIS
⚖

The GR goes east out of Grambois and takes the Mirabeau road. At the end of the village, after the cemetery, it turns right, passes beneath the portico of the municipal stadium and, on a forest path, climbs the west side of the Défens mountain (map ref M). Two kilometres after the spring and the ruins of La Valbonnette, go right (south) on a hunters' path across the wood. It goes down to the Mirabeau plain. Pass between the farm of La Turquerie and the road from Mirabeau to Grambois, which you avoid. The Limites track emerges at the D135. From this road as far as Les Auquiers (399 on the map), the road is private. Hikers should thus be quiet and careful. The GR9 follows the D135 southwards; 200 metres further on, it turns left to pass the Ferme de l'Etang. Cross the farmyard with the kind consent of the owners, then turn sharp

3:30

right to the south, and at the end of the cultivated fields go left (east) again. The GR skirts north of the hamlet of Le Suyet, crosses the valley of Traou-de-Loups, then turns across the wood in a general east-south-east direction and gains the D973 near Mirabeau.

MIRABEAU
🍷 ⚓

17th century château with four towers, which belonged to the father of Mirabeau, the most famous orator of the French revolution, and in this century to the writer Maurice Barrès.

West of the village the GR takes the road down the Vallon du Rivet which descends towards the River Durance and comes out at the N96.

0:30

Detour *15 mins*
RELAIS MIRABEAU
🏨 🍴 🚌

Go left (north) on the N96 for 600 metres.

The GR follows the N96 to the right to the Pont de Mirabeau.

Pont de Mirabeau
(Mirabeau Bridge)
242m

Cross the bridge. Start from here, because of construction work on the motorway, the markings for the GR9 are not definite as this guide goes to press. Follow carefully the temporary markings, which will alter according to the demands of the construction work. Go left on the N552 in the direction of Saint-Paul-les-Durance, then take the D11 to the right for 500 metres. At the second bend, take a cart track on the right which narrows as it reaches the cultivated land of La Davouste (l'Adaouste) farm. Walk along by the fields to reach a road which, 1 kilometre further on, rejoins the D11 (there is a car park here). Follow the D11 to the right (south). One kilometre further on, near the ruins of the farm at La Neuve, is the junction with the future GR99a (IGN ref 421).

1:15

Junction with the GR99a

To the right (east), the GR99a — planned as the link between the GR9 and the GR99 — heads towards Saint-Martin-des-Pallières via the Grande Bastide (a *gîte* in the district of Rians, administered by the Regional Association for the promotion of the Pays du Verdon). The GR9 continues to follow the D11 southwards for another kilometre. Then it takes a dirt track to the right (west, then south-west) which crosses the wood of La Fautrière. The road is gradually less defined, threads amidst the

0:45

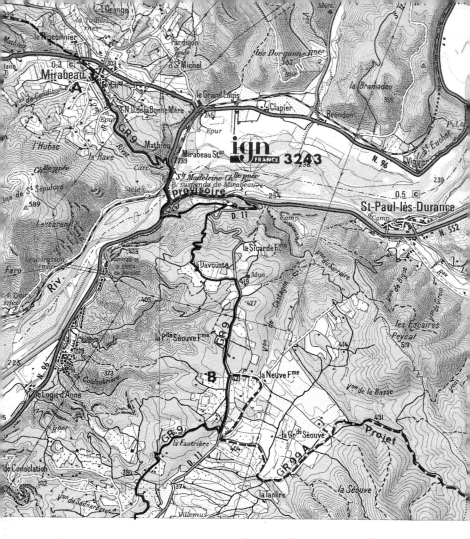

garrigue, briefly alongside a field of almond trees then again through the bushes. It passes near a *borie* (drystone hut) in an area of weekend cottages, cuts across a number of paths and reaches a major path at the top of the Vallon de Saunaresse (Sadnaresse), called the Chemin de la Reynaude. Go sharp left along this one to reach the D11 in the hamlet of Bèdes.

Fifty metres further on, the GR turns right at a transformer, and takes the Chemin de la Gouiranné, bordered by drystone walls, through an area of holiday cottages. It turns into a stone-paved mule track, and ends up at

Bèdes
353m.

0:30

JOUQUES
🏠 ⛺ 🍴 🍷 ⛲
🚌

*Village built in tiers up a
rocky hill oriented east-west,
exposed at mid-day but
sheltered to the north by a
cliff that used to serve as a
rampart. Along the crest,
from east to west, ruins of*

Le Pigeonnier, in front of the château of the
archbishops of Aix-en-Provence. Walk down
the picturesque old streets as far as the D561
to reach Jouques.

The GR crosses the D561, goes along by the
car park, then crosses the bridge over the
Réal and immediately proceeds south on a
road which climbs Le Deffend hill. Here you
will find a ruined chapel and a view over the
village.

the Château Vieux (Old Castle); church of Notre-Dame de la Roque; château and gardens of the archbishops of Aix-en-Provence; 15th century church.

Ruined chapel

1:15

The road crosses part of a new housing estate and descends gently as far as another road. Take this left (south-east) for about a hundred metres, then turn right on to a dirt track, where the sandstone slabs have been worn away by cart wheels. Cross a glade to reach a resurfaced road at a bend; take this left for 50 metres, then continue straight ahead to the south on the grassy road to Le Cannet. The GR arrives at a verdant area where there are weekend cottages, and meets the bank of the ancient Verdon canal, which takes water to Aix-en-Provence; walk along the bank to the left for 300 metres. Turn right, cross a bridge, and then after a great curve you will meet up with the D11, south of the area of La Payanne and not far from a hair-pin bend.

Main road (D11)
361m

2

Take this road to the right (west, then south) for 7 kilometres. It is a narrow, winding road that rises amidst a wood of oak saplings; it passes the Château du Grand Sambuc, now a medical teaching centre and a breeding place for pheasants, then crosses the Grand Sambuc pass. It then descends a gentle slope, passes the ruins of the Petit Sambuc and runs beside a field on the left. At the end of the field, turn right (west) at the point where the road enters the gorges of the Vallon des Masques.

Vallon des Masques

0:45

The GR takes the chemin rural de France path to Le Petit Sambuc, recently widened as a defence against fires, which rises to the Seauves plateau. It heads west, passes beneath a high-tension wire, and after crossing areas of sparse vegetation and stands of oak saplings, it arrives at a crossroads where it meets the Carraire d'Arles.

Carraire d'Arles
600m
This was the ancient route between summer and winter

The GR goes left (south-east), again passes beneath the high-tension wire (you will see the pylon 50 metres south, on the edge of the plateau), then turns directly right (south) on a

0:30

pasturage in the Crau Plain and Haute-Provence.

VAUVENARGUES

🏠 🍴 🍷 ⚖ 🚍

430m
The 14th and 16th century château is an opulent building with turrets and a fine park. It belonged to Pablo Picasso, who is buried in the park. Not open to visitors.

2:20

Prieuré de Sainte-Victoire

⌂

888m
5th century origins. 17th century buildings restored by the Friends of Sainte-Victoire, and occupied for the last 25 years. Monks' garden. Entering by the west gate, you will find on the left the chapel and the prior's quarters, next to which there is an altar sheltered by vaulting. A secular pilgrimage known as 'Lou Ramavagi de Santi Vitori' takes place here annually on the 24th April, or the nearest Sunday.

0:15

Croix de Provence

Lookout post for the forest fire service. The first cross

well-marked track which zigzags between stunted, thorny scrub-oaks. Finally it descends a steep slope along the D10 (from Vauvenargues) into the little valley of La Cause, opposite the château of Vauvenargues and the renowned Montagne Sainte-Victoire.

The GR bypasses the village of Vauvenargues and goes right (west) on the D10 for 2 kilometres, as far as the area of Les Cabassols (357 metres). Near Les Cabassols, the GR leaves the D10 for a dirt road on the left, the Chemin des Venturiers, which is shady in summer. Along this route you can see the local markings in green. The road, bordered by private land, goes by the hamlet of Les Cabassols on the right, and makes a gentle descent to cross the torrents of La Cause and l'Infernet (although these are often dry). Then it rises to reach a small peak, when the slope gets steeper, and after twisting through the wood, you reach the end of the forest path at an altitude of 710 metres. The GR climbs the left bank (west side) of the valley of La Croix, passes near a shelf and makes a long loop to arrive at the Prieuré de Sainte-Victoire (priory).

The GR skirts the priory, passes beneath the enclosure and the chapel, then winds up the side of the mountain and passes beneath the Croix de Provence.

The GR takes an easterly direction and proceeds now on the slopes, now along the crests, and passes beneath the Garagaï,

1:15

was erected here in the 16th century; the present cross, 18 metres high, is the third (1875). Splendid panorama over the whole of Provence: in the west, *from the Alpilles to Le Ventoux;* in the east: *as far as Les Maures and L'Esterel;* to the north, *in fine weather you can see as far as the Dauphiné.*

Baou de Vespré
1010m
The 'baou' or 'baû' is a steep rock forming a terrace; it is the central summit of the massif, and is marked by a cairn.

1:30

Pic des Mouches
1011m
This is the culminating height of the massif, with a panorama explained on the viewpoint table.

0:30

Oratoire de Malivert
775m

1

PUYLOUBIER
⌂ ⌂ 🏕 🍴 🍷
🚃 🚐 🚋
380m
Ruined medieval château; Romanesque church, restored in 1860, containing a beautiful altar from the Ursulines of Aix-en-Provence; institution for the disabled of the Foreign Legion at the château Le Général; Roman ruins in the area.

1:30

where the rock face is pierced by a huge natural tunnel. Keeping east along the crest, the GR reaches the sign for Sainte-Victoire (969m), with its belvedere (not marked on the IGN map). The GR then crosses the arid level of La Crau (not marked) to reach the Baou de Vespré.

Warning: there are various high paths up to the Pic des Mouches — do not attempt these in bad weather.

You will then reach the Col de Subéroque (938m, not marked) and the Col de Vauvenargues (921m), which gives a view over the south face. The GR drops down to skirt the Baou de l'Aigle, then climbs again to the Pic des Mouches.

The path descends to the east, passes near rock which has caved in, the Cagoloup *garagaï*, with shallow shafts, ignores some marked paths that are not well-maintained, then returns to vegetation and descends to the Oratoire de Malivert. All along this route hikers should be extra careful because of the fire risks.

The GR goes along the top of the Église valley, passes beneath a high-tension wire and reaches a hilltop through scrub-oak. Then, on a good path which curves slowly east on a hilltop, the GR descends to Puyloubier.

The GR arrives in the village of Puyloubier at the Place Damasse-Malle, and takes the Grand Rue to the right (west), coming out at the Place de la Mairie. It leaves the village by the D57 in a south-westerly direction. At a fork, take the D57b to the right; 1 kilometre further on, turn left on a dirt road which runs alongside a telephone wire and then by the edge of a wood. At the far end of the wood, there is a small dip on the left. Pass the Gavot farm (a ranch), then cross the Baraque vineyards to reach the N7. Follow this left (east) for 400 metres as far as the Logis de la Colle.

Logis de la Colle
278m

1:30

TRETS
Ⓗ ⌂ ▲ ✕ ⟁
🚊 🚌
242m
Situated at the foot of Mount Regagnas. Ancient Roman town of Trittia.
Remains of ramparts with two open doors in the square towers (14th century); 15th century château; church, dominated by its unfinished 15th century bell-tower; synagogue with 13th century façade; old houses lining narrow streets. The area produces cereals, wine and melons.

2

Please note: *If you want to stay at the priory hostel of Saint-Jean du Puy, first obtain the keys from M. Léon Baille, in the Brest neighbourhood of Trets.*
☎ *42.61.49.14.*

This path may go back to the Gallo-Roman era, as the environs of Saint-Jean-du-Puy are rich in remains from this period, notably stone slabs.

Turn right (south) along the D57 and follow it for about 1.5 kilometres. Near a large oak-tree (IGN ref 249) veer left as far as the hamlet of Cadenet. The GR goes underneath the A8 motorway and reaches the young River Arc, which it crosses. The route proceeds south as far as the D56, which it takes to the left, alongside a railway line, then crosses the line. Enter Trets by the main road.

The GR crosses the town of Trets, passing the *mairie* on the right. Take Rue du 1er Mai on the left of the *mairie*. Via a maze of little streets in the old town, you arrive in front of the church, and then leave the town by the Saint-Jean gate. Go south down the Rue Cambon, which becomes the Chemin de Saint-Jean; from here you can see the bell-tower of the hermitage of Saint-Jean-du-Puy (map ref H).

You pass an oratory of St John the Baptist preaching, built on a rock with a well-preserved panel of carved wood at its base. The road, until this point surfaced and wide, now narrows (though it is still usable by cars) then becomes a footpath leading into a copse.

The GR continues uphill, soon reaching a second oratory, that of Saint-Zacharie, surrounded by bushes and rocks, and then a third, of St John baptising. Finally it gains a wide tarmacked road, the Chemin de la Légion étrangère (the Foreign Legion), linking the D12 (Trets–Saint-Zacharie) with the summit of Saint-Jean-de-Puy. Take this road left (east), passing the entrance of the estate of La Grand'Boise; before the bend on the right, take the rocky road going up on your left, cutting across the Chemin de la Légion to reach the former priory of Saint-Jean-du-Puy, where there is a hostel (map ref H).

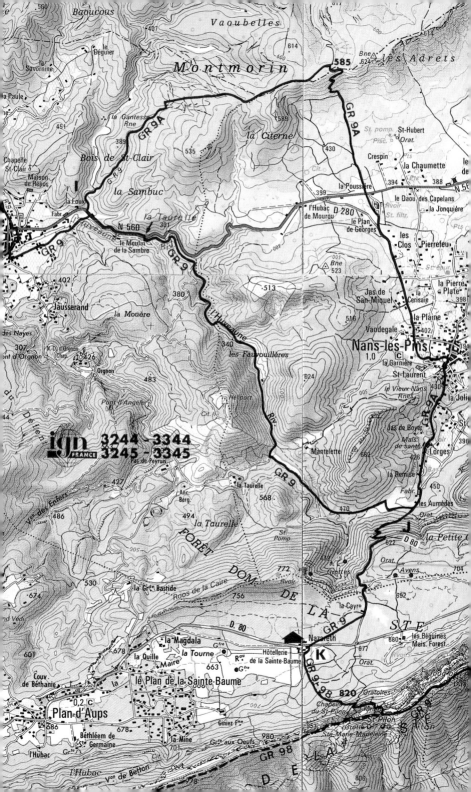

PRIEURÉ, (PRIORY) OF SAINT-JEAN-DU-PUY

⌂

657m
(Indicated as an 'oratoire' on the IGN map.)
First mentioned in 1153, when the priory belonged to the bishop of Marseilles. The last hermit left the area in 1891. It then fell into a very dilapidated state, and became a listed sites in 1938. Since 1960, the Friends of Saint-Jean-du-Puy has endeavoured to restore the buildings. Hut accommodation is available — see Trets for access details.

1:15

The GR leaves the oratory of Saint-Jean-du-Puy by a footpath running south-west through boxwood; it descends a gentle slope into the *maquis*, then the slope gets steeper. The route heads south and reaches a small, verdant valley. Here, water erosion has caused the path to cave in; follow the bed of the stream, then regain the path on the left bank. The GR passes beside a channelled spring, then unfinished construction works, crosses an old green clay quarry, and once again joins the bed of the stream. It soon leaves this for a path which runs beside farms and houses, and joins the D85. Go left on the D85, and via the Courts Louis-Blanc — planted with handsome plane-trees — you will reach the village of Saint-Zacharie.

SAINT-ZACHARIE

▲ ✗ ⟁ ⚒ 🚌

265m
Romanesque church, founded by the Cassianites in the 7th century and reconstructed after the Saracens left; pagan altar dedicated to Jupiter, on show at the mairie; *famous pottery.*

0:45

From the Cours Louis-Blanc, the GR goes left along a little street which leads to the N560; take that left (east) for 50 metres, then the Rue de la Révolution, which heads south towards the Huveaune. After the schools, go right on the narrow Rue Raspail which overlooks the river and ends at a square. Descend to the left to cross the river by the transport bridge. About 50 metres on from this bridge, near a fountain, turn left on to a road that is surfaced for a while and then becomes a dirt track which climbs the left bank of the Huveaune; it crosses a stone bridge to meet up with the N560 near the La Foux inn (map ref I).

HÔTELLERIE DE LA FOUX

⌂

278m
This is where the alternative route GR9a begins; it rejoins the GR9 south of Nans-les-Pins, near Les Aumèdes.

Alternative route from Hôtellerie de la Foux to south of Nans-les-Pins (GR9a). The GR takes the N560 left (west) for 100 metres, then to the right the road called the Chemin de la Reine Jeanne.

1:45

Queen Jeanne was very young, only 17, when she became Queen of Provence (1343–82); she often used to take this road which stretches as far as Saint-Maximin. These days it is a rutted path, often overgrown.

The path enters a small valley; where it forks, go up to the right, keeping north-east, and pass a ruined sheepfold (380 metres). The GR keeps climbing, gradually eastwards and then north-east again to join the ancient Nans road, which it follows to the right (south). It arrives in the vicinity of Les Adrets.

Les Adrets
585m

1:15

NANS-LES-PINS

⌂ **Å** ✕ ⟁ ⚓

🚌

394m
Detour *20 mins*
ruined château.
Take the path to the right
which mounts to the ruins of
the 13th century château,
and gives a fine panoramic
view. Below it you can see
the traces of the ancient
fortified village.

0:30

Les Aumèdes
450m

1:45

The road makes a twisting descent to gain the N560, which it crosses in the vicinity of La Poussière, and joins the D280 in the vicinity of Plan de Georges. Take this left for 2 kilometres, then where it turns left (east), continue straight ahead (south), again on the ancient Nans road. It heads towards Le Vieux Nans, traces of which are still visible at the foot of the ruined feudal château. The GR bends left (eastwards), draws near the village, passes a fountain (with abundant fresh water) and reaches La Font Vielle, which leads to the church at Nans-les-Pins.

The GR takes the Rue de l'Église as far as the chapel of Notre-Dame-de-Miséricorde.

The GR takes a road to the left (south) which climbs through open country, and then through woods. You walk alongside the buildings of the Lorges nursing home, and, 300 metres further on, leave the surfaced road leading to a house for a footpath to the left through a pinewood; 700 metres on, after La Remise, you join a well-marked path coming from the Nans-les-Pins–Sainte-Baume road. Going south on this path you rejoin the standard route of the GR9, near Les Aumèdes.

The GR arrives on the right from the Hôtellerie de la Foux.

The GR9 takes the N560 to the right for 700 metres. It passes the Auberge du Vieux Moulin de la Sambre (Sambuc) (the Old Mill of la Sambre Inn), and proceeds as far as the entrance to the Domaine de la Taurelle (322m), a state property managed by the ONF. Turn right to cross a bridge over the River Huveaune, and climb up the left bank to the Lazare springs (not marked on map). There are channelled springs and the area is planted out in plane trees. Still on the left bank, the GR follows a forest track, then fords the river (this is usually dry) and climbs the right bank, crossing the Huveaune again to reach a little pinewood. About 300 metres further on, once more on the right bank, the valley narrows and the path rises in order to avoid a previous path eroded by water. You then arrive at the place where the Huveaune disappears. The valley widens out, the GR reaches a path which it

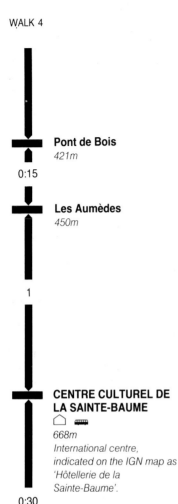

Pont de Bois
421m

0:15

Les Aumèdes
450m

1

**CENTRE CULTUREL DE
LA SAINTE-BAUME**
668m
*International centre,
indicated on the IGN map as
'Hôtellerie de la
Sainte-Baume'.*

0:30

Detour *45 mins*
PLAN D'AUPS
*12th century Romanesque
church.
Follow the D80 westwards.*

Carrefour de l'Oratoire
820m
*16th century oratory, and a
mission cross.*

Detour *20 mins*
**Grotte de la
Sainte-Baume**
(Sainte-Baume cave).

leaves in order to cross a ford of tree trunks and return to the left bank. It runs alongside a field, passes near a spring, and arrives at the forest track of La Taurelle, which it takes eastwards. This track rises gently to cross the river one last time, by a wooden bridge.

A little further on, a chain prevents motor vehicle access to the Domaine de la Taurelle. The forest track meets the ancient Chemin de Nans, south of Les Aumèdes.

On the left you will find the GR9a coming from Nans-les-Pins and the La Foux Inn. The GR9 takes the Chemin des Rois (the Kings' Road) to the right (south-west) and, in a series of bends, after a steep climb reaches the D80. Take this to the right, and cut across several corners to reach an ancient sheepfold (676m), a very old building, which is an annexe of the Sainte-Baume cultural centre. In the vicinity of La Cayre, take the right-hand fork (south-east) and cross an oak wood to reach the Sainte-Baume cultural centre, which is on the D80 (map ref K).

The route for the GR9 is the same as that for the GR98 as far as the Col du Saint-Pilon, see p. 171.

To the east of the Sainte-Baume buildings, the GR passes an enormous oak, marked with arrows, then between two pillars to bypass the cemetery and follow an avenue of chestnut trees. It then enters a forest. On the Chemin des Pèlerins (Pilgrims' Way), it rises gently towards a heap of moss-covered rocks, surrounded by luxuriant vegetation; the slope gets steeper and you reach the Carrefour de l'Oratoire (Oratory Crossroads) by means of a wide stairway.

To the left, a wide road descends to the Nans fountain, the last place for water before the springs on the other side of the Col des Glacières.

Detour, see left: Follow a wide road westwards; it is marked in brown and climbs as far as the steps leading to the cave marked as 'Grotte de Sainte-Marie-Madeleine' on the map.

0:30

From the terrace there are views of the forest, the Plan d'Aups, the Aurélian mountains and the massif of Sainte-Victoire. At the foot of the terrace is the entrance to the cave where Marie-Madeleine did her penance; the relics of the saint have been placed here, and the cave turned into a chapel. The votive feast is on 22 July.

On a wide, gently sloping path, the GR proceeds up the mount, passing the ruins of the chapel of the Parisians (a precarious shelter), then between two fences, where there are beautiful views to the east over the north face of the Béguines, and to the west over that of Saint-Pilon above the cave. After several twists beyond the forest, you reach the Col du Saint-Pilon.

Col du Saint-Pilon
950m
(See description on p. 195.)

0:40

At this point (map ref L) the GR9 meets the crest and separates from the GR98, which runs to the right (west), takes 10 minutes to reach the Chapelle du Saint-Pilon (994 metres), a little shelter near a viewing table.
The GR98 proceeds west over the ridges towards the Pic de Bertagne, the Ange pass, Cassis, and the Calanques massif as far as the gates of Marseilles. (See p. 207.)
The GR9 goes to the left, in an easterly direction, following the crest on its southern slope. On a rocky track across the *lapiaz*, a cracked, chalky plain, it goes past several summits, including the Joug de l'Aigle (the eagle's perch).

Joug de l'Aigle
(Jouc de l'Aigle)
1118m
Surmounted by a cross.

0:35

You walk near a deep pothole (18 metres), then reach the Béguines signpost.

Signal des Béguines
1148m
A geodesic reference point, the highest peak in the chain, and a view the same as that from the viewing point at Saint-Pilon.

0:30

The crest now drops down considerably. At the entry to the valley — facing the south-east — the GR abandons the crest route to go along the valley, and then crosses it. On the other side of the valley, the GR takes the cliff road, descending a gentle slope which offers a fine view of the ice wells which supplied Marseilles and Toulon until the turn of the century. It reaches the end of the range, where the slope gets steeper and you reach a passage between two rocks, inappropriately named the Col des Glacières.

Col des Glacières
851m
There is a spring 50 metres to the right.

Warning: the GR then crosses the estates of Font Frège and Font Mauresque, which are private property. Hikers are asked to observe the marked route with great care.

The GR enters a forest — there are springs in the gully — and follows a patchily grassed path, not very clear in places, which at a bend joins a wide cart track.

You will be able to see the slender tower of the Château Delestaing or Font Mauresque.

Take this track to the left (north); 300 metres further on, at a corner, the GR turns sharp right to skirt the château of Font Mauresque, then descends, passing a spring and a lavender field, and catches up with the earlier path. It spans first one stream (which rises in the valley) then another, more important, Le Latay (map ref 660). Climb up the left bank, where the footpath widens to become a cart track. Soon afterwards, you will pass a stone slab on which is inscribed 'Signes 1 h 30' (1 hr 30 mins). The path leaves the stream and goes south across a plateau, a lavender field, then a pinewood. It then cuts across a good road (IGN ref 670) to take a rutted short-cut across the wood and up a small pass. A horizontal path joins another below, in the Vallon de la Caou with its poplars. Fifty metres further on, you will find a spring between the stones of a retaining wall. The GR runs alongside the wall and the gully to reach the farm at Taillane.

Ferme de Taillane
676m
squat house flanked by two crumbling Saracen towers; also a sheepfold, water and possibly accommodation (M. Moutte).

Warning: in the valley the path is overgrown with vegetation and isn't usable; follow the markings carefully. Do not walk over the cultivated land; keep dogs on leashes.

The route proceeds along by the fields and meadows, then rises, passes underneath a high-tension wire and arrives at the 'collet' Notre-Dame or the Col de la Croix Taillane (also called the Saint-Jean pass), where there is a ruined oratory. The GR descends a steep hill and crosses an area rich in fossils. The slope lessens and you cross a small canal, which is the overflow of the channelled spring of the Raby (430 metres). The road, almost flat here, arrives in sight of the Château-Vieux. Then it drops down, passes between two rocks at an oratory, and comes to the bridge over the Raby waterfall. This road, now surfaced, crosses an area of cultivated land dotted with houses. It crosses the stream in a narrow pass by the Vieux-Moulin bridge, and reaches the first houses of Signes.

1

1:15

SIGNES

ⓗ ▲ ☗ ▭

340m

the district of Signes is a largely wooded area. It is an excellent place to stay and a good departure point for a number of walks. Since the 12th century, the feast of Saint Jean and Saint Eloi has been celebrated on 23 June with procession, floats and fireworks. At the chapel of Saint-Jean they make an offering of lemons. Castellas from the Ligurian era (c.600 BC); ancient walls; Gallo-Roman site; clock tower in the marketplace; church of Saint-Pierre, with 15th century doorway; the 15th/16th century chapel of Saint-Jean.

1:15

The GR9 goes south across the village of Signes to arrive at the D2. This is a junction with the GR99, which heads north towards Mazaugues and the Verdon. The two GRs head south; 200 metres on, the GR99 continues in the same direction towards Toulon (6½ hours from Signes). The GR9 turns left (east), crosses a housing estate, then takes a little-used surfaced road across the vineyards. First of all it crosses a branch of the Provence canal, where the waters of Verdon feed Toulon and the Vaud littoral, and then a stream which is often dry, the Latay. The path proceeds in the same direction and passes several weekend cottages; it turns right and crosses another branch of the Provence canal, called the 'Bretelle de Solliès', which feeds the Solliès plains, Hyères and the Vaud coast east of Toulon. Straight after the bridge, turn left, go along by the canal to bypass a vineyard, and meet the old road from Revest to Signes, which has become a path of beaten earth. It rises imperceptibly as it crosses a wood, bordered by drystone walls, as far as a practically flat road.

Detour *1 hr 30 mins*
Montrieux forest route

Detour, see left. A path marked in yellow goes off on the left; it comes to the bank of the canal, crosses the bridge over it, briefly goes along below the canal, and passes near the stud farm at the Moulin du Gapeau (Gapeau windmill), then the Lucrèce. In the area around Les Arguilles (needle rocks) de Valbelle (map ref P) it rejoins the GR9 on the Montrieux forest route. This itinerary avoids 200 metres each of ascent and descent.

Go right along this road to reach the Bastide de l'Hubac (map ref O).

Bastide de l'Hubac
404m
This is in ruins, and the route passes below it.

1:45

Winding across undulating terrain, the GR gradually wends its way up the hillside beneath handsome oak-trees. Having gained a little more height, the GR then proceeds almost level to the south. There are beautiful views northwards over the convent at Montrieux, Méounes, the Loube massif and Les Arguilles de Valbelle. Finally it reaches the highest point, the Barre de l'Eoure.

Barre de l'Eoure
640m

At this point, the GR leaves the road.

Detour, *30 mins,*
Colle de Fède.

*The road continues south
and passes the Clos de
Peiron vineyard to join the
GR99, at the bend where it
begins the climb to the Colle
de Fède (IGN ref 825). (See
dotted line on map.)*

0:30

After it leaves the road, the GR descends
steeply to the bottom of a small valley, until it
reaches a charcoal-burner's hut, near La
Lucrèce Ruines.

Charbonnière
600m

Take the fork left (east-south-east) and descend the hillside amidst the dense vegetation.
After a double loop, you will reach the bottom
of a valley; the footpath becomes rutted, then
widens; the slope eases off and you will
encounter yellow markings.

The route marked for the GR9 and the yellow
path crosses an oak grove and, 300 metres
on, enters the forest by the forest path of
Montrieux.

1

Montrieux forest route
420m

Alternative route from La Lucrèce Ruines to
Pas de Truébis. You can follow a route marked
in blue which is an alternative to the GR9; it is
less hilly and allows you accommodation in
Méounes-les-Montrieux. It meets up with the
GR9 when it reaches the Barre de Cuers, at
the Pas de Truébis (map ref Q).

Chartreuse de Montrieux

Follow the blue markings left along the
Montrieux forest route northwards as far as the
convent of Montrieux-le-Jeune, where there
are springs, a fountain and shelter.

*Charterhouse (Carthusian
monastery) founded in 1118
at Montrieux-le-Vieux to
replace a Cassianite
convent; transferred to this
spot mid-12th century.
Provence has several
renowned Charterhouses,
but only that of Montrieux
has survived numberless
ordeals, wars, persecutions
and pillaging; the monks
returned here in 1928. The
monastery houses great
treasures (relics, altars,
tombs), not open to visitors.*

1:30

From the Chartreuse de Montrieux-le-Jeune,
you can take the track marked in blue which
crosses Le Gapeau and leads to Méounes-les-
Montrieux.

MÉOUNES-LES-MONTRIEUX

310m; situated on the D554 (Toulon–Brignoles), this is an excellent place to stay and a good base for a number of excursions. 16th century Gothic church, with marble altar; two cherubs flying off a tomb, 17th and 18th century statues of Saint Omer and Saint Delphine from Chartreuse de Montrieux.

From Méounes, the blue markings take a southerly direction, cross the Selves plain and rejoin the GR9 when it reaches the Barre de Cuers, at the Truébis pass, 1½ hours from Méounes.

I

1

Truébis pass

There is a little dam here, intended to conserve rainwater for use against forest fires. To the right, in a grassy hollow, a cedar was planted at the inauguration of the GR9 in 1972 on the 25th anniversary of the footpaths association.

Valbelle Ruins
570m
precarious shelter; cistern with dubious water.

1:20

BELGENTIER
▲ ✕ ♈ ⚒ ▰▰▰
159m
16th-century château (visitors not allowed); well-known tannery; factory for preserving olives.

Detour *2 km*
AUBERGE DE PACHOQUIN
◠
North of Belgentier, on the D554, there is the Auberge de Pachoquin, tel: (94) 48.98.13; the coach timetable makes it possible to stay there overnight and return the next morning.

1:30

The GR9 now follows the Montrieux forest route eastwards, as it threads its way through the dolomitic area of Valbelle, with its needle rocks and other strange rock formations. You go through the Porte de Valbelle ('gates'), then rise in several loops, allowing good views of the needles, and reach a tree with a moss-covered plaque.

Keeping to the forest route, cross a cedar plantation on the Valbelle plateau, then pass near the ruins of the farm at Valbelle on your left.

The GR9 continues east on a cart track. It crosses a plateau, skirts a large field and arrives at the end of a rocky ridge, which is the Pas de Belgentier (538 metres). The GR descends steeply down a rutted path. After several tight bends, it reaches the little valley of La Font de Vin, crosses it and proceeds as far as Belgentier.

There is a fountain in the village square in Belgentier. You are advised to get water here as it is difficult to obtain later. From the square, the GR heads east along the Avenue de Cuers, at the post office. The street becomes a surfaced path running above an irrigation canal, and then rising gently to an oratory (not marked on map). After a sharp turn left, take a mule track which, between drystone walls, rises to a projecting ledge on the side of the valley. Crossing the scrubland, the GR climbs the length of the valley then, making a loop southwards, crosses it to reach a small peak (400 metres) via a steep slope. Here there is a viewing platform and forest track. The GR turns sharp left (north), climbs a knoll, crosses

a ledge, and, keeping north, joins the ancient Truébis mule track. By a steep track with hairpin bends, the path sometimes cut into the rock, the GR reaches the Truébis Pass.

Trébis Pass
(Pass de Tréubis)
560m

Detour *30 mins*
Méounes-les-Montrieux

1:30

Detour, see left. Follow the blue markings north-west. They lead to Méounes-les-Montrieux via the Selves plain. This route, which also passes the Chartreuse de Montrieux-le-Jeune, rejoins the GR9 on the Montrieux forest path at an altitude of 442 metres, near the ruins of La Lucrèce. It is an alternative route to the GR9 (see page 178).

After the Pas de Truébis, the GR goes north-north-east along the Barre de Cuers. All these walks offer fine views to the south over the Cuers plain, the Maures and the Mediterranean. The hilly route, across *maquis* and oak groves (via IGN ref 698), then descends to reach the Pas de Cuers.

Pas de Cuers
592m
Detour *1 hr 30 mins*
CUERS
⌂ ✗ ⏐ ⚰ ☎
⎚
139m
Follow the yellow markings south.

1

From the Pas de Cuers, the GR rises then drops to the Pas de Brusquet (610 metres). Climb up again to reach the Pilon de Saint-Clément.

Pilon de Saint-Clément
705m (map ref R).
There is a geodesic signal, and an immense, impressive panorama. (See below)

0:30

From the Pilon de Saint-Clément, descend north-west along a track that is not much marked but which soon becomes clear, although rutted. Head towards an electric pylon on the north side of a rocky ridge, to gain a ledge about 100 metres before the pylon. Turn sharply east on the Pas de L'Empereur (603 metres). You leave the Barre de Cuers, descending a pretty, old path bordered with trees, then rutted. Several metres from the path there is a spring which has been harnessed to serve the Domaine de Saint-Clément and La Bigue farm. The path straddles a small slope created by the opening of a forest path. Follow this path right (south-east). Having passed by La Bigue farm,

View from Pilon de Sainte Clement

To the south: the Cuers-Pierrefeu vineyards and the valleys of the Maures massif; the Mediterranean with the Hyères Islands and the semi-island of Giens; Mont Fenouillet; the Colle Noire (Black Gap); Toulon and its harbour and Cap Sicie.

To the south-west: in the background lie Mont Faron, the Coudon and Mont Caumes, and the Grand Cap; nearer to hand, the Morières massif and the Jas de Laure chain.

To the west: nearby is the Puméningond plateau, behind that, the Agnis massif and the Sainte-Baume; the gap of Signes allows sight of the Mediterranean and La Ciotat with the Bec de l'Aigle and the Calanques massif.

To the north-west: the mountain chains of Aurélien and Sainte-Victoire; further away, Mont Ventoux and the Lure mountain.

To the north: in the foreground are the vineyards of the Garéoul plain, the ruins of the Chateau Forcalqueiret, and Loube mountain; to the east, the Saint-Quinis ridge, the *castellas* of Saint-Sauveur and the Department of the Var, with a mass of villages and, like a backdrop, the mountains of Le Cheval Blanc (the White Horse), Le Mourre de Chanier, Margès and Barjaudes. In clear weather you can see the Pic de Bure, the Trois Évêchés (The Three Bishoprics), the Pelvoux massif, and the Ailefroide (Cold Wing) with the Coup de Sabre (Sabre Blow).

To the north-east: the giant of the Var, Le Lachens (1715 metres), Le Teillon, La Bernarde, Le Grand Coyer, Mont Mounier and the Tende Gap, with all the peaks of Le Mercantour.

Crossroads with the D43
423m

0:45

ROCBARON
383m

1:10

you will reach a crossroads with the D43 (423 metres).

At this point, cross the D43 and go north-north-east along a forest track which winds between copses and vineyards and then comes to an oak grove; a little further on, follow a wire fence eastwards. Cross a dry stream then, once again among vineyards, join the D12 near Rocbaron. Having crossed the D12, the GR passes near two wells and the Rocbaron wine co-operative warehouse.

The GR does not go through Rocbaron. It takes a north-easterly direction near a mission cross encircled by cypresses. It follows a rutted, pebbly path bordered by drystone walls. After climbing along the small valley and crossing it through a sparse wood, you reach a little pass (441 metres). Go along the ridge then over the north slope; within sight of a large scree, climb a steep slope to reach a pass (map ref 571) in the vicinity of Les Terres Blanches (White Lands). The GR descends to the bottom of a broad valley, cuts across a cart track (520 metres) and passes the wells of

Sauzède, in a grassy hollow. There is a fine oak tree here — a good place to camp. In a dip, take a path south-south-east which, amidst small oaks, arrives at the edge of the rocky ridge of the Pas de la Porte-Étroite (496 metres).

Pas de la Porte-Étroite
(Narrow Gate pass)
496m.
This offers a view over the plain, and shelter under the rock.

The route scarcely diverges from the ridge, except to avoid a few overhanging places; it provides beautiful views over the Maures. At the axis of the Thèmes basin to the north is situated the Pas de la Foux (map ref S).

Pas de la Foux
450m

This is a very narrow passage.

Detour *1 hour*
PUGET-VILLE
🏠 ✕ 🍷 ⚘ 🚂
🚌
190m

Detour, see left: A path marked in yellow crosses the Pas de la Foux. If you follow it south, you will pass the hamlet of La Foux and will then reach Puget-Ville. You will find several springs along the way.

After the Pas de la Foux, you leave the ridge and, by a short, steep descent, head north towards the Thèmes basin. You arrive at a cart track bordering cultivated fields; 100 metres to the left there is a spring on the edge of the wood. Follow the path on the right, marked in yellow, at the edge of the wood; go as far as the beginning of the private land signalled by a notice and a chain. Although the yellow marking continues northwards, the GR goes straight ahead on a wide track that rises up through a green oak wood as far as a 'collet' (450 metres). This allows passage over the rocky ridge; the path descends steeply, offering fine views over the plain, the vineyards of Puget-Ville and the Maures.

Castellas were established in this region — 13 in all — from which the invaders' road to Provence was surveyed and defended.

When you reach a ledge, the first crossroads appears, which you cross in an easterly direction; you will encounter a second crossroads, then a third (296 metres). The GR turns right (south) to descend into a small valley. Go as far as the surfaced lane, and take that to the left (east). You pass a number of weekend cottages, a cemetery and, via the Rue de l'Égalité, you arrive at Carnoules on the D13.

CARNOULES
🏠 ✕ ⚘ 🚂 🚌
220m

The GR goes east across the village of Carnoules, passes the Place Jean-Jaurès and, at the north-east corner of the church, turns

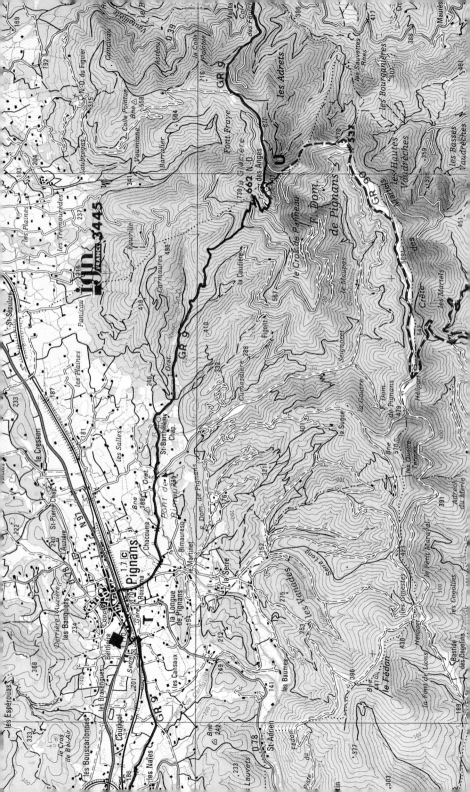

1:20

PIGNANS
✕ ⓨ ⚒ 🚂
170m

2:30

Source de la Glacière
662m
There is a fountain here, and
you are advised to get water
as there is none available
until the hamlet of La Haute
Cour, which is 5 hours' walk
away.

0:30

right (south) to join the N97 at the edge of the village. Take the surfaced by-road opposite, bordered on the right by a garden with greenhouses and on the left by a stream; it passes beneath the railway bridge, twists between gardens and orchards, and crosses the stream. After curving left, it proceeds alongside the railway line, crosses it beneath a bridge and rejoins the N97 at the entrance to the village of Pignans.

Avoiding Pignans, the GR runs along the verge of the N97; 500 metres further on, it turns right (south) on to the Notre-Dame des Anges road, and passes under the railway bridge. It then takes the forest road of Cros de Paneau eastwards (not shown on the map), to arrive at the Pont de Rimauret or Rimauresq near an oratory (180 metres). Do not cross the bridge, but take the Rimauret track eastwards. It climbs the right bank of the stream, then skirts north of the restored chapel of Saint-Barthélémy, built on a hill and surrounded by cypresses. The GR crosses a one-way bridge over the confluence of the ravines of the Rimauret and Notre-Dame des Anges. There is a permanent spring 15 metres to the right, south of the bridge and hidden in the greenery. Soon after the bridge, on the left, you pass an oratory; you climb the left bank of the valley of Notre-Dame des Anges, where there is a second oratory, then ford the stream at the entrance to the little valley of the Caudière (252 metres). The GR leaves the Carmaures track on the left and climbs south-east up a hill to join the ancient pilgrims' way stretching between the oratories. It crosses an age-old chestnut grove which occupies the sides of the valley of La Glacière and, in several twists, reaches the surfaced forest road. It takes this left for 100 metres, as far as the spring of La Glacière (661 metres); also called the 'Source de la Vierge' (the Virgin's spring).

The GR twists its way upwards among the chestnut trees along the lane lined with restored oratories; it cuts across the road twice and reaches Notre-Dame des Anges.

NOTRE-DAME-DES-ANGES

⌂

767m

From the esplanade there are extended views over the Maures and the Mediterranean, and the upper Var and the Alps to the north. In the far distance, you can see the watchtower of the forest fire service. Sanctuary or hermitage of Notre-Dame-des-Anges, a chapel that may be pre-Romanesque, enlarged in the 19th century; in front of it is a building for pilgrims, forming a cloister, managed by the Friends of Notre-Dame-des-Anges. Tradition has it that Nymphe, the sister of Maximim (the first bishop of Aix-en-Provence) retreated here and sculpted the statue of the Virgin which is venerated today. There are five days of pilgrimage: the Mondays of Easter and Pentecost, 2nd July (the Visitation), most importantly 8th September (the patronal festival), and 21st November (the Presentation).

Col des Fourches

534m

This pass, situated on the D39, allows passage from Gonfaron on the N97 (8 kilometres) to Collobrières, in the heart of the Maures, on the D14 (12 kilometres). Famous for centuries-old chestnut trees and marrons glacés.

This is the departure point for the GR90 south-east, which leads to Le Lavandou, via Collobrières. (See page 00.) The GR9 skirts the buildings and chapel of Notre-Dame-des-Anges to regain the surfaced road. Turn right (south-east) 200 metres further on, on to a road which goes alongside a wire fence, then passes underneath a telephone line. Go down the steep slope to reach another road, which is the ridge road, called the 'Piste Marc-Robert'. Follow the 'Piste Marc-Robert', the only usable road in an easterly direction, then cut across two wide bends, going over a hilltop to arrive at the Col des Fourches.

From the Col des Fourches, the GR9 takes the D39 left (north). At a hairpin bend 400 metres on, it goes right (east) on the Piste Marc-Robert, which is the only authorised track. This rises imperceptibly over the north slopes of La Petite Sauvette (631 metres) and of La Sauvette (780 metres). To the north, there are beautiful glimpses of the whole of the Var, and further, from the Alps of the Dauphiné as far as the Italian frontier and the Argentéra massif. The track reaches the small peak of Rouve-Gavot (620 metres). The track, which is shored up, goes down the south slope, along the valley of Valescure and drops down to the Cros de Mouton pass.

Col de Cros de Mouton
556m

1:15

Camp de Bérard
628m
Memorial to Marc-Robert here (a young fireman killed in 1973).

1

Haute-Court
370m
Spring and pool at the entrance to the hamlet, where you will also find shelter.

1:30

LA GARDE FREINET
320m; once a large industrial village (raising silkworms, making corks, exploiting the resources of the chestnut groves) with 2500

0:50

After the Cros de Mouton pass, the GR, keeping to the Piste Marc-Robert, skirts the heights of the valley of the Garrière to meet the Pré des Masques crossroads (607 metres). It rises past the Rocher Blanc, veined with pure quartz. The route makes a great sweep north, arriving at a 'collet' from which you have a good view of the Maures and the gulf of Saint-Tropez. From this point, follow the Maures ridge (Crête Serrière), crossing the Piste Marc-Robert several times. Hikers are asked to follow the GR markings and not the road, so as to make the maintenance of the footpath easier. You will pass near a reservoir, then arrive in the vicinity of Camp de Bérard.

A little further on, leaving a track on the left which descends southwards, continue along the Piste Marc-Robert as far as the Col de la Court (597 metres), at the entrance to the valley of La Court. Here the GR leaves the road on the right to cross the clearing and join a footpath. Take this east to descend into the little valley of La Court. Ford a stream (448 metres; the spring is a little higher) and, on the left bank among the chestnut trees and the cork-oaks, you descend to the hamlet of Haute-Court.

From the hamlet of Haute-Court, the road becomes surfaced and, leaving the hamlet of Basse-Court on the right, goes through the chestnut trees following the bumpy terrain. It passes near several springs and below the villa du Val Verdun (450 metres) to reach a small peak (511 metres). Among pines and chestnut trees, the GR passes the foot of the Trois Bresques and descends northwards as far as the D558, which it joins opposite the chapel of Saint-Éloi, the youth hostel and the holiday village of Les Aludes. Follow the D558 to the left for 200 metres to reach a crossroads at the entrance to La Garde-Freinet.

The GR does not go through the village of La Garde-Freinet; at the crossroads, south of the village, it takes the D75 to the right for 3.5 kilometres. This road winds among the chest-nut groves in a north-easterly direction. At the point where it heads north towards the Col de Vignon, the GR goes right, along the Piste de la Galine.

inhabitants in 1880. Today it survives only because of the tourists, attracted by its beautiful location.

Piste de la Galine
350m
(Map ref W).

2

Following the Piste de la Galine, you pass directly beneath La Basse-Lioure and, in a great loop to the south, descend and cross the little valley of Pourcasse. The track rises again, passes Les Amandiers, a ruined farm, and crosses a little valley in a tight curve, where there is a run-off. The rocky track follows the lie of the land to reach a small peak (248 metres) when it cuts across a road. Now a sandy track, it continues east on the northern slope, providing a good view of the Plan de la Tour, and meets up with the D44 beneath the Bastide Neuve.

La Bastide Neuve
184m

1:30

Cross the D44 to take a road that runs alongside a vineyard, then enters a grove of oaks. The GR rises, skirting to the west of the San-Peire (416 metres), then going south as far as a small peak (185 metres) which offers a beautiful view of the gulf of Saint-Tropez and the Mediterranean. It makes a winding descent as far as a ruined farm, then it becomes rutted and heads towards a valley, which it crosses. The GR follows along the right bank, and between the vineyards the road becomes suitable for vehicles. It passes the hamlet of Les Lions Sablonneaux, and winds among mimosa, between a stream and the wire fence of a camping ground, until it reaches a gate. Here it crosses a stream, the Bagarède, by a one-way bridge to arrive at the D244. Take this road left for 600 metres, as far as the N98.

SAINT-PONS-LES-MÛRES
🏠 ⛺ ✕ 🚌
In the hamlet of Grimaud, 300 metres from the sea. Sainte-Maxime, a summer and winter resort, is 7 kilometres to the east. To the west is Port Grimaud, and 7 kilometres away is Saint-Tropez, with its historic interest and present-day world fame.

The GR9 Jura-Côte-d'Azur comes to an end here.

WALK 5

Col du Saint-Pilon
950m

Chapelle du Saint-Pilon
A small 17th century cubical building with a porch (precarious shelter) built on the site of a pillar ('pilon') supporting a statue of Mary Magdalene. Small terrace with fine panorama of forest, Régagnas mountain, Saint-Jean du Puy, Aurélian peaks and Sainte-Victoire. To the south: *Embiers Islands, mountains of Toulon with Mount Caumes, Grand Cap;* further east: *continuation of Sainte-Baume chain. Beyond these, the Pre-Alpes of Haute-Provence. There is a panoramic map just beside the chapel.*

1:20

IGN map ref 1035

0:30

Citerne de l'Escandaou
(Escandaou water tank)
900m
This is the only place with a permanent water supply before Cassis, with a shady site nearby.

0:30

While the GR9 heads east, the GR98 goes west, more or less following the line of the crest. It reaches the Chapelle du Saint-Pilon.

From the Chapelle du Saint-Pilon, across the *lapiaz*, cracked, chalky ground, the fairly uneven, windswept footpath more or less follows the line of the ridge westwards, then, at the level of the radio transmitting station, meets a wide depression sloping south to reach a valley. Proceed over bumpy ground on the great slabs of limestone in the direction of the army radio tower. The GR reaches a fence around antennae and a heliport. It runs alongside this fence on the south side for 200 metres. The path meets a road and then reaches the point numbered 1035 on the map, near a low rocky ridge.

The GR leaves the Department of the Var and enters that of the Bouches-du-Rhône. It descends towards the south slope of the chain, keeping generally west-south-west, and meets a broad valley. The route continues in the same direction until it encounters the brown markings in the direction of the Pic de Bertagne, on which stands a radar station whose white globe is visible from all directions. At these brown lines, the GR9 heads directly south down a valley and reaches the Citerne de l'Escandaou.

The GR descends a steep slope as far as the Vallon de l'Aigle. It heads south-east then, over level ground, it arrives at La Bergerie du Deffend (a ruined sheepfold).

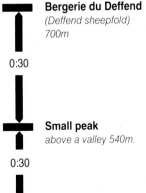

Bergerie du Deffend
(Deffend sheepfold)
700m

0:30

Small peak
above a valley 540m.

0:30

A little after the sheepfold, the GR once more heads south, and descends amidst scrub-oak. To the north, there is a fine view of the jagged Roque Forcade, dolomitic needle rocks, and of the great mass of rock which is the Pic de Bertagne, surmounted by the white radar globe. Follow a cliff road which arrives at a small peak above a valley.

Go left and then, in a great loop, return west along a wide forest track in the direction of Le Brigou and Mont Cruvelier. Pass beneath a high-tension wire. After it passes a recently built house, the GR arrives at a small peak and a ruined sheepfold.

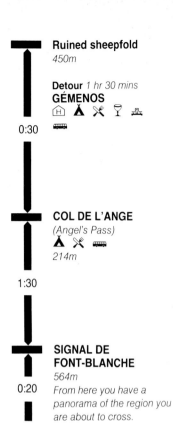

Ruined sheepfold
450m

Detour *1 hr 30 mins*
GÉMENOS

0:30

COL DE L'ANGE
(Angel's Pass)
214m

1:30

SIGNAL DE FONT-BLANCHE
564m
0:20
From here you have a panorama of the region you are about to cross.

Detour, see left. A little before the sheepfold, take a forest path to the right (westwards) which skirts Mont Cruvelier to the south.

After the ruined sheepfold, first descend southwards, then turn east, passing the cabin of Le Brigou, now a little house; then, heading south again, you will reach the Col de l'Ange (map ref b).

Take the D1 opposite (south) for 1 kilometre. At the crossing, continue ahead on the D3d for 1.5 kilometres. After a bend, where there is a large wooden sign indicating the forest of Font-Blanche, leave the road and turn right on to a road which climbs up to a pass (481 metres). Here, turn left (south) along a road. Pass by a metal pylon then, on a path, climb up to the Signal de Font-Blanche.

From the Signal de Font-Blanche, descend south-west on a wide, cracked chalky path. This ends in a track suitable for vehicles 500 metres further on. Turn right (west). You pass Le Cabanon du Marquis de Villeneuve.

CABANON DU MARQUIS DE VILLENEUVE

520m
0:30
Old hunting cabin, provides basic shelter.

The GR descends imperceptibly and heads towards a building surmounted by a lookout, which is the Cabanon des Gardes (the wardens' hut).

Cabanon des Gardes

484m
0:30
This offers basic shelter.

Go over a pass, and reach the N559a after descending a gentle slope.

PAS D'OUILLIÉR

330m
Follow the N559a to the right (north) for 300 metres to find refreshments.

0:30

At the Pas d'Ouille cross the road and climb the bank to follow alongside the B52 motorway (Marseilles–Toulon), on a broad cliffside road. In sight of the north toll, cut across fallow land, and follow the access route to the toll as far as the N559a. Proceed along this on the right-hand side; 200 metres further on, join a little road that crosses the motorway by a tunnel to get to the south toll. Cross a small open space used for parking, go left on a road which goes through a pine grove to come out at the access road for the south toll; take this along the inside of the crash barrier as far as Le Pas de Bellefille.

PAS DE BELLEFILLE

195m

0:45

At the Bellefille pass, cross the N559 and take a footpath which climbs south across plantations, then a south-west path which heads towards a ventilation shaft from the railway tunnel of the Toulon–Marseilles line. After a few metres the GR leaves this behind on the left, together with a kind of arch, and takes a path to the right which rises towards the ridge to attain the summit called 'La Couronne de Charlemagne' (Charlemagne's crown, 331 metres). From the summit, follow the ridge until you reach a gap, descend to the left across a cracked, chalky *lapiaz* as far as a *collet* or collar; here, take an almost horizontal path which leads to a broad depression in the main ridge, at the foot of the rocky shelf forming La Couronne de Charlemagne. You should have a good view of the Baie de Cassis from here. Beyond the depression, the GR takes a forest track to the left, passes near a water tank built to aid fire-fighting, then it leaves the track for a short cut on the right, and returns to the track to reach the Baou de la Saoupe.

Baou de la Saoupe

(Saoupe Mountain)
344m

The GR takes the access road to the relay station, and goes down to a crossroads called the Pas de la Colle (214 metres). Descend the

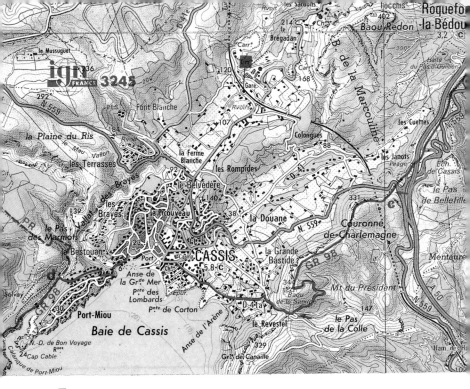

Television relay station. Marvellous views over Baie de Cassis and eastern part of the Calanques; on the right the Baou Canaille (in Provençal, 'Cap Naïo') rise 400 metres above the sea. They are also called the Falaises Soubeyrannes, and are the highest cliffs in France, indeed in Europe.

CASSIS

Warning: *you must purchase provisions and water here, because until La Madrague de Montredon, perhaps 30 kilometres and about 10½ hours' walk, the hiker will find almost nothing in the way of food and water. On this route there is no accommodation available, and camping is forbidden.*

Avenue des Crêtes; 500 metres further on, turn left round a very sharp corner, and the slope gets steeper in the Avenue de Revestel, which passes above Anse de l'Arène. You then come to the Avenue de l'Arène, which passes the stadium and arrives at a crossroads where the markings stop. You enter Cassis via the rue de l'Arène.

In Cassis, follow the Quai des Baux to its end, then, leaving the port, go right, along the Avenue Amiral Ganteaume which climbs west; you will pass above the beach at Bestouan and near the village car park. At the signpost indicating Les Calanques — Port Miou — Port Pin, you will find the markings again. The GR98 goes right, down the Avenue des Calanques, and reaches a crossroads.

1

0:25

Crossroads
(map ref d)

Alternative route from Cassis to Col de Candelle. Go north-west at the crossroads, following the blue markings which go via Mont de la Gardiole to rejoin the GR98 at the Col de Candelle (or Chandelle) taking 3 hours and 10 minutes.

Detour *30 mins*
LA FONTASSE
⌂

Detour, see left. From the crossroads mentioned above, follow the blue markings (dotted line on map) over the Pas des Marmots to where it meets the tarmacked forest road from the Col de la Gardiole. Take that road left (south) for 400 metres, as far as the youth hostel.

COL DE LA GARDIOLE
⌂

From the crossroads with the blue markings, the GR goes left as far as the car park of the *calanque* at Port-Miou; it leaves the quarry on the right for the path to the north of the *calanque*, goes along by the harbour buildings, then climbs a cliffside road as far as a *collet*. Go down the terraces formed from rocks and the roots of pine-trees to cross the *calanque* of Port-Pin, where there is a shingle beach. The GR ascends a winding path, then a track, to the Plateau de Cadeiron (150 metres), where it cuts across a wide forest path.

Plateau de Cadeiron
50m

Detour *5 mins*
REFUGE DE PIOLET
(Piolet hut)
⌂

Detour, see left. Take the wide forest path to the left (south) as far as the Refuge de Piolet. It has room for 10 people, but does not have water. It is situated at the edge of a cliff on the *calanque* of En Vau, the prettiest of all the inlets.

Detour *35 mins*
LA FONTASSE
⌂

Detour, see left. Follow the wide forest path to the right (north) until you reach the youth hostel at La Fontasse.

The GR crosses the plateau and draws near the ridges overhanging the *calanque* of En Vau. (See page 205).

Go down a succession of rocky steps and slippery slabs, cross a wide crack or 'chimney', to reach the beach of En Vau. Several metres beyond the beach, the GR climbs north up the forest path, which plunges into the En Vau valley, passes the foot of the little needle

The Calanques

The *calanques* are narrow, deep inlets, like fjords, where the sea steals in between high cliffs; by extension, the name calanques ('calanco' in Provençal) has been given to the whole limestone massifs which extend over more than 20 km between the sea — to the east, south and west — and the road in the north connecting Marseilles with Cassis. The massifs have an astonishing variety of forms: tortuous little valleys, a tangle of ridges, slender peaks, vertical cliffs, sometimes smooth, sometimes striated — making the landscape appear desolate, wild and chaotic, and difficult of access. In the whole area there are not ten places of 100 square metres which are flat or uniform. But the nature of the rock itself is the same everywhere: tight-grained limestone. It has been chiselled by erosion; at the feet of the dazzling white sheer walls there are heaps of scree.

From La Provence des calanques *(Société des Périodiques Larousse).*

rock of En Vau, then the Grand Aiguille (tall needle rock), and then a third (the Alp Hutli) to reach the Portalet crossroads. Go left here, along another forest road which climbs the steep slope up to the Col de l'Oule.

Col de l'Oule
160m

From the Col de l'Oule, the GR follows the forest road west, as far as the Oule wells, now dried up, then heads south to descend into the valley of the Oule (not marked on the map). It then turns sharp right to climb the steep slope of a gorge — some sections are particularly steep — and reaches a hilltop beneath a pass.

1:30

In the rockface you can make out some natural openings, and, rising above the water table, the elegant rocky needle of the Eissadon.

The GR follows the edge of the cliffs of Le Devenson, which tower more than 300 metres above the sea, and the *calanque* of the same name with its little rocky island, Le Dromadaire (the dromedary). This *calanque* can only be reached by the climbers' paths or by sea.

Along this route there are various crosses and plaques to the memory of climbers who have been victims of accidents.

The GR goes over the Col du Devenson, the departure point for a number of climbers' paths, then, via some rocky passages, climbs to the highest part of the cliffs (321 metres), and goes down again to the Col des Charbonniers.

Col des Charbonniers
(Charcoal-burners' Pass)
250m
Situated at the western extremity of the Vallon Les Charbonniers. Magnificent views over the Val Vierge

From the Col des Charbonniers, by a succession of stone slabs and mounds of scree, climb north until you get to a footpath, and take a sharp left turn along it. More or less horizontal to begin with, it then descends to cross a valley. After this, climb on good paths and over scree as far as the Col de la Candelle.

0:45

which ends at the calanque of the Oeil de Verre; large rocky slabs of La Lèquè; cape and calanque of Morgiou, and the needle rock of the Grand Candelle (Chandelle).

Col de la Candelle

443m

This pass is situated just below the needle of the Grande Candelle (Chandelle). It is the junction with the blue markings coming from Cassis via Mont de la Gardiole. Its line westward is the same as the GR98 until the meeting with the forest path (215 metres).

0:30

From the Col de la Candelle, the itinerary takes a cliff road in a north-west direction, then goes down the path called the Treize Contours over scree and reaches, above a valley, a forest path (215 metres).

Forest path

215m

0:40

The route waymarked in blue, which goes off to the right, rejoins the GR98 at the Col des Baumettes, 1½ hours along the ridge. The GR98 takes this path south; 200 metres on, it turns right to go down a footpath which, after a bend, heads south-east; then it leads to a rocky indentation, with a view over the Calanque de Sugiton. The slope gets steeper as the path crosses a heap of large stones. Go over a small rocky pass to reach the Toits de Sugiton, and go along the foot of the cliff. You will arrive above a cove that is almost always in the shade, and then at a shingle beach which is the Calanque de Sugiton.

Calanque de Sugiton

This has a little rocky island, called Le Torpilleur (torpedo boat).

0:40

After the Calanque de Sugiton, the GR climbs the opposite slope by means of a 3 metre metal ladder. It skirts Cap de Sugiton, and a rocky passage with slippery slabs enables you to reach the left bank of the Calanque de Morgiou. A cliff path takes you to Port de Morgiou.

PORT DE MORGIOU
🍷 ☎

Go through the port, then take a path on the right bank which leads into a rocky passage and passes by a needle rock. This path, called 'Corniche du Renard', rises imperceptibly to the crest of Cap de Morgiou. Do not go as far as the point, but head north-west to scramble over scree and gain the crest above the Calanque de Sormiou. The slope decreases

1:30

PLAGE DE SORMIOU
✕ ▲ ☎

0:30

Col des Baumettes
(Map ref g).
182m
This is a junction with the
blue route coming from the
forest path (215 metres) —
via the Col des Escourtines
and the ridges — where it
meets the GR98 again.
The route, marked in blue,
goes along the GR98 as far
as the Col de Cortiou.

0:30

Detour *15 mins*
QUARTIER DES
BAUMETTES
⌂ ⌂ ✕ ♆ ⚓
🚌
From the Col des Baumettes
a red-marked route
descends north to the
neighbourhood of Les
Baumettes.

Col de Cortiou
245m

2

and you will arrive at a crossroads called
'l'Étoile' (240 metres), south of the Le Baou
Rond. From this crossroads, the GR takes a
track to the left, which runs west-south-west
along the base of a rocky ridge, crosses steep
screes, then after some tight bends, you reach
the bottom of the valley and the fishermen's
port. Go along the port to reach the beach at
Sormiou.

The GR climbs the Sormiou valley again, on
the right, and twisting its way through the
rocky ridges, reaches the Col des Baumettes.

From the Col des Baumettes, the itinerary for
the GR98 runs east, reaching the Col de
Sormiou (182 metres), where it cuts across the
road from La Cayolle to Sormiou and keeps
west along the path which rises to the Col de
Cortiou.

Alternative route from Col de Cortiou to La
Madrague. The blue markings take you via the
Marseilleveyre Massif, and the Sommet de
Béouveyre, rejoining the GR98 in the valley of
l'Escalette, near La Madrague.

The GR98 takes a rocky course to the left, then
the sentier des douanes (the customs' path)
which descends westward, skirts a hollow then
joins the coast path. You will pass near the
Calanque de l'Escu, skirt the Calanque du
Podestat, then after passing several needle
rocks, you arrive at the top of the Calanque de
Marseilleveyre. Skirting that, the GR makes a

broad sweep, passing above the Calanque de la Mounine, and goes along the coast. Then, on stone slabs, it climbs to the semaphore to reach the Calanque de Callelonge to the north.

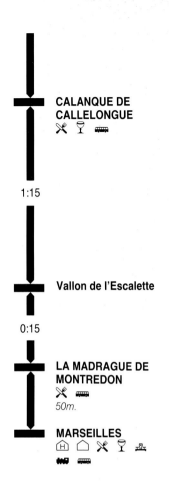

CALANQUE DE CALLELONGUE

1:15

Go down the only street in Callelongue, then at the far end follow the little valley, and climb left up the slope of the Marseilleveyre Massif to reach a path (the Sentier du Président, dedicated to the memory of A. Pellice, a great hiker and remarkable administrator, president of the Société des Excursionnistes de Marseille. It was built to link up with La Madrague de Montredon). This coastal path provides fine views of the littoral. The GR goes along the west slope and over a pass. After several ups and downs, it arrives at the 'collet' of the Vallon de l'Escalette.

Vallon de l'Escalette

0:15

This is a junction with the blue route coming from the Col de Cortiou via the Marseilleveyre Massif and the Sommet de Béouveyre. From the small peak, the GR98 descends north to La Madrague de Montredon.

LA MADRAGUE DE MONTREDON

50m.

The GR98 finishes here at the gates of Marseilles. You can reach the centre of Marseilles by bus.

MARSEILLES

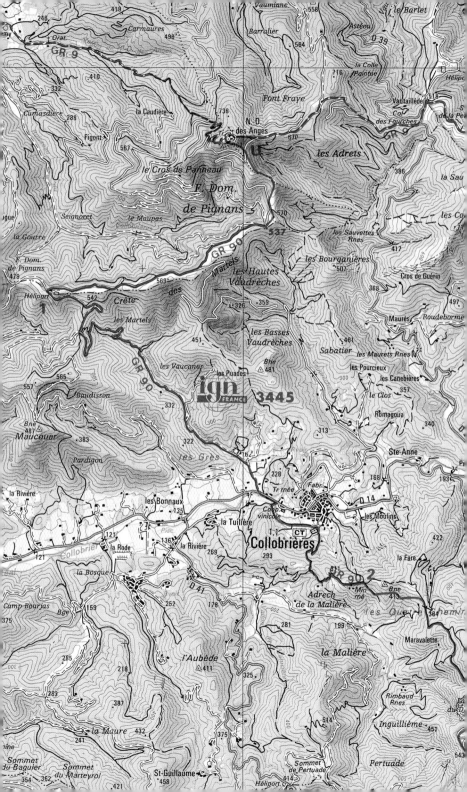

WALK 6

The GR90 begins at the belvedere of Notre-Dame-des-Anges (map ref U), which overlooks the south part of the forest, and is visible from a distance because of its firewatch tower and a television mast. It goes up hill and down dale, over the Maures massif, passing through some remarkable chestnut groves before it reaches the sea at Le Lavandou.

NOTRE-DAME-DES-ANGES

⌂

780m

0:25

Facing the entrance to the hermitage, you will see that the GR9 goes off to the left, while the GR90 passes between two walls and descends at the corner of some old outhouses. After crossing terraced slopes, it winds first among chestnut trees then bushy heather, and comes out on the road at a major crossroads. To the left (east) is Confaron, and to the right Pignans (north) and Collobrières (south). The GR goes left (south-east) along the bank beside the road, and makes its way among the cork oaks, following the boundary of the national forest marked in white/green/white and an old blue line painted by the *syndicat d'initiative* of Collobrières. The path overlooks the valley of Les Adrets, where there is a handsome restored farm, and goes to the right again above the Collobrières road. On the left (east), a good road descends to a stream, the Grand Vallat, and the D39 which links Gonfaron with Collobrières. The GR climbs up opposite (south) and zigzags between the oaks, coming back to the road called the Crête des Martels.

Crête des Martels

537m
View of
Notre-Dame-des-Anges.

0:50

The blue line descends left (south) into the little valley of Vaudrèches. The GR takes the Crête des Martels route westwards for 1 kilometre. (This is also called the Piste Marc-Robert after a young fireman who was killed in a forest fire in 1973.) You reach a crossroads. To the left, the road descends into the valley of Vaudrèches towards Collobrières, 8 kilometres away. Follow the road to the right along a plantation of conifers, and head west for a steady descent. Ignore a track going down to the right, the GR continues across the forest. On the way, you will have beautiful glimpses of the Carnoules plain and of Puget-Ville in the north. Then you arrive at the heliport crossroads (map ref 1).

Héliport
520m

0:25

Piste de Vaucanes
428m
Hut offering precarious
shelter.

1

COLLOBRIÈRES
150m
This is the capital of the
Maures. Chestnuts provide
the main source of activity in
the village, which
manufactures marrons
glacés. *Cork used to be*
equally important, but today
this industry is declining.

0:50

The reservoir and heliport for the DFCI (Défense de la Forêt contre les Incendies: forest fire protection) overlook the crossroads. To the right, a track goes towards Pignans and the GR9 (there is a rain gauge below the track). The GR90 goes left (south-east) for 1.5 kilometres on the road through a forest of cork oaks. After a big loop, it arrives at another crossroads.

To the right, there is the Piste de la Saute, where the footpath 'Des Balcons de la Côte d'Azur et de la Provence' will go, and the Piste de Baudisson which leads to the D14, 7.5 kilometres to the south. The GR90 skirts to the right of the hut and follows (south-south-east) the Piste de Vaucanes which, after two great loops, meets the stream of the same name. The GR fords the stream and follows the right bank. The valley widens for a little and the track again crosses the stream, which then runs through a gully. The cork oaks give way to chestnut trees. After passing a ruin which leans against an enormous cypress, you arrive in the vicinity of Les Grès. Notice the well preserved windmill on the left. The GR goes left, skirting a large vineyard and comes out at the D14, at the entrance to Collobrières.

Follow the D14 left for 350 metres towards the village, then turn right before the wine co-operative, which produces the *Côtes de Provence*. The GR descends, skirts a sewage plant and, having crossed the river, 'Le Réal Collobrier', climbs the left bank and follows it along. You will occasionally encounter the yellow markings of a former PR, no longer in use. By a path which is shady in summer, you will arrive at the other end of the village. Pass the police station, cross the bridge over the Perrache stream, and turn right beneath the esplanade of the parish church. After the cemetery, the path rises steeply, passing two farms. It goes over the top of the hill through a cutting (there is a little shrine cut into the rock on the right), and goes down several metres towards the valley of La Malière. It abruptly turns left on to a wide path through a grove of chestnuts (with a hut below) and twists its way upwards to the south-west. You thus arrive at a small peak, beneath an oratory dedicated to Saint Pons (311 metres). The GR then heads right (south-west) through heather and cistus and passes near an age-old cork oak to reach a ruined mill (map ref 2).

Moulin ruiné
(ruined mill)
381m
View over Notre-Dame-des-Anges and Collobrières.

The footpath widens and goes between pine trees to meet another footpath (the former walking route, marked in blue), coming on the left from Collobrières. After this intersection, the GR rises steadily east and enables you to see in the distance the Destéou ravine. The path overlooks the valley of La Malière and its chestnut forest, passing south of La Fare farm, and descending, arrives at the intersection called Les Quatre-Chemins (364 metres). It carries straight on opposite, and becomes a wide path which passes through a typical Mauresque forest, amidst chestnuts, many of which are a hundred years old. You can reach the valley of La Malière in 15 minutes, by taking a path to the right (west). A good climb through the undergrowth brings you to a surfaced track on the Plateau de Lambert.

1

Plateau de Lambert
474m

Follow this surfaced track to the left, towards a eucalyptus wood, past two standing stones on your left. The standing stones or 'menhirs' of Lambert, are grey sandstone columns about 3 metres tall. After a plantation of Douglas pines, on the left, there is the junction with the PR path marked in yellow, leading to the Chartreuse de la Verne and the Grand Noyer dam, where it rejoins the GR90 (see dotted line on map).

Detour *2 hrs 15 mins*
Chartreuse de la Verne
422m

Detour, see left. Take the path marked in yellow to the left (east).

While the PR goes left (north-east) after the Lambert standing stones, the GR90 goes across a eucalyptus wood and descends to the right, towards a stream, the Desteu (Destéou).

1:30

In a wild ravine, where access is dangerous, the Destéou of Collobrières eddies and cascades between deep banks. It takes the name La Malière as it reaches the Domaine de la Malière, renowned for its modern Gothic chapel, of a very austere design.

The GR then crosses the stream beneath the small dam, equipped with a *limnigraphe*, to measure the flow rate of water. It takes a footpath alongside the gulf, which you can leave in order to reach the two viewing points indicated by red and white dots, 30 metres away. The route changes direction abruptly. The GR heads south across the *garrigue*. It returns to the track, leaves it several times to cut corners, then follows it north-east for 2.5

kilometres. Then turn right (east) on to a forest path which descends quite steeply to end at the foot of the Montagne du Faucon, on the southern slope, at a height of 546 metres (map ref 3).

Mont Faucon
546m
View over the Dom forest and the Mòle plain.

The footpath sets out below the platform and descends steeply southwards, amidst heather and thorny broom. It skirts left around a large rock. Turn sharp left (east), and taking a footpath which begins as a ledge down through bushy heather you will meet a cart track, which passes below a ruin. Turn left and, a bit further on, leave the road which goes right towards the Petit Noyer farm. The GR goes directly north again for 800 metres, crosses the last chestnut grove on this route (please do not pick the chestnuts), fords the Petit Noyer stream and arrives at the ruined farm of Le Grand Noyer. Leave that path and go right, down a footpath which runs beside a cultivated field and, amidst oaks, fords the Grand Noyer stream. You will meet up with a track a little further on; it comes from the left above the Retenue du Grand Noyer (dam).

Retenue du Grand Noyer
260m

This is the junction with the PR path which, taking this track east, leads to the Chartreuse de la Verne in 2 hours. The GR descends to the left on the embankment of the dam and zigzags between the oaks, on a wide path for a moment, then fording the stream (Le Petit Noyer) once more. It runs alongside the fence of the INRA (l'Institut National de Recherche Agronomique: National Institute for Agronomy Research), better known as the Ruscas Arboretum (no visitors allowed) and arrives at the N98 at the Baraque de Bargean.

Baraque de Bargean
82m
Precarious shelter.

Cross the N98 linking Hyères and Cogolin, and take the wide cart track opposite, which crosses the stream, the Bargean, and enters a forest. The GR cuts across a firebreak track then descends to the right and turns sharp left (east) to ford a stream, the Campeaux. It then enters on the most luxuriant part of the route, where enormous trails of ivy have overgrown the great pine trees, creating a shadowy area sprinkled with flowers — violets, narcissi, orchids, asphodels, Maures lavender etc. Leaving the path, climb steadily up the footpath on the right (south) amidst bushy

1

0:30

0:50

heather, which ends in tight bends to emerge on the Piste de Dom-Sud. Take this track to the left for 1 kilometre among the oaks, as far as the Col du Pommier.

Col du Pommier
(Apple Tree Pass)
168m

At the crossroads, ignore the track on the right which leads directly up to the Col de Landon, and go right ahead on the good path which follows the hillside ˙and overlooks the valley where a stream runs, the Femme-Morte (Dead Woman). The GR proceeds through an oak grove amidst flowers, and crosses the stream just after a dam (possibly good shelter). The path rises steadily, parts from the stream for a moment, then comes back along its left bank. The valley narrows, you cut across several tracks, and continue on more or less flat ground. The stream widens at the point where the path runs alongside an imposing mass of rock. Looping twice, the path gains height, leaving the stream on the left. It becomes a footpath through undergrowth which, in tight bends, meets the Col de Landon.

1:15

Col de Landon
380m
View over the Femme-Morte valley, Bormes and the littoral.

At the crossroads of the tracks, the GR rises left (south-east), following the boundary of the national forest (marked out in white/green/ white); it threads between rocks, then arrives on a plateau, at the Pré de Roustan (468 metres). Turn right (south) on a wide cart track, which crosses the plateau amidst the heather. It passes under a high-tension wire, once more turns right and descends gently, crossing a field of cistus. It rises again in the direction of an electric cable and goes left around La Pierre d'Avenon.

0:30

Pierre d'Avenon
(d'Avenoun)
(Avenon stone)
443m
'Avenoun' (Lat. avena, Fr. avoine (oats)). In recent times the plateau was given over to cultivation of oats. This is a geodesic reference point, and offers a view over the sea, stretching from the Gulf of Saint-Tropez to Toulon, with the imposing mass of Mont Coudon.

Warning: the GR crosses private property here; do not stray from the path, keep dogs on their leashes as there are herds in the area, and respect the property. When you reach the road from Bormes to Canadel, follow it to the right for 100 metres. Then go left on a narrow footpath below the road, descending towards the Landon valley. Again pass beneath the high-tension wire to reach a good road. Go right, passing a spring, and you will arrive at a ruin. The path (or track) descends in curves to the valley, ignoring another path on the right. From this point you will encounter signboards. Ford the stream, the Landon, and climb up as far as a crossroads. Here, continue straight

1:10

ahead along by a field of vines, passing one of the quarries which furnish the famous 'pierre de Bormes' (Bormes stone), which is much sought after for decorating houses. The GR crosses a grove of mimosas and, after a big loop (round a second quarry), ends up at the D41, near the cemetery. Take this road left for 750 metres to enter Bormes-les-Mimosas.

BORMES-LES-MIMOSAS

This village is listed as the first in its class in France. It benefits from an exceptional micro-climate, and is especially famous for its mimosa woods. The mimosa festival takes place on the second Sunday in February. Steep little streets, with vaulted passageways, stairs, nooks and balconies in flower; church of Saint-Trophine; chapel of Saint Francis; 12th century chapel of Notre-Dame-de-Constance (350 metres up), which takes an hour there and back along the oratory way, and offers a panoramic view; fort de Brégançon, summer residence of the President of France; arboretum of Le Gratteloup on the N98, between the road to Collobrières (D41) and the GR90, which crosses the N98 at the Baraque de Bargean.

0:50

The GR arrives at Place Gambetta, passes the *Syndicat d'initiative* then climbs the Rue J. Aicard and Rue G.-Peri, turns after the post office and enters the town park. It leaves this by the stadium road, in a big loop, and leaves the road after the roundabout to thread through the rock by a small path on the left, which comes out at a housing estate. It then passes by the houses, crosses the road again and enters the stadium; follow the markings carefully and the SI signboards, go round to the left and avoid the hand-ball area. The GR emerges once again amidst housing estates, but allows sight of the port of Le Lavandou. It then takes a pretty path (the old town road between Bormes and Le Lavandou) and arrives at the road, passes the electricity station and ends up on the N559, near a telephone box at the entrance to Le Lavandou. The GR ends here.

LE LAVANDOU

INDEX

The many different kinds of accommodation in France are explained in the introduction. Here we include a selection of hotels and other addresses, which is by no means exhaustive — the hotels listed are usually in the one-star or two-star categories. We have given full postal addresses so bookings can be made.

There has been an explosive growth in bed and breakfast facilities (chambers d'hôte) in the past few years, and staying in these private homes can be especially interesting and rewarding. Local shops and the town hall (mairie) can usually direct you to one.

Details of bus/train connections have been provided wherever it was possible. We suggest you refer also to the map inside the front cover.